Study Guide

Corporate Finance

Scott B. Smart
Indiana University

William L. Megginson
University of Oklahoma

Lawrence J. Gitman
San Diego State University

Prepared by

Joseph Vu
DePaul University

THOMSON

SOUTH-WESTERN

Australia · Canada · Mexico · Singapore · Spain · United Kingdom · United States

THOMSON

SOUTH-WESTERN

Study Guide to accompany Corporate Finance

Scott B. Smart, William L. Megginson, Lawrence J. Gitman

VP/Editorial Director:
Jack W. Calhoun

VP/Editor-in-Chief:
Mike Roche

Executive Editor:
Mike Reynolds

Senior Developmental Editor:
Trish Taylor

Freelance Developmental Editor:
Joanne Butler

Production Editor:
Tamborah E. Moore

Senior Marketing Manager:
Charlie Stutesman

Senior Media Technology Editor:
Vicky True

Media Developmental Editor:
John Barans

Media Production Editor:
Mark Sears

Manufacturing Coordinator:
Sandee Milewski

Printer:
Globus Printing

Senior Design Project Manager:
Michelle Kunkler

Cover Designer:
Ramsdell Design, Cincinnati

Cover Images:
© Photo Disc

For permission to use material from this text or product, contact us by
Tel (800) 730-2214
Fax (800) 730-2215
http://www.thomsonrights.com

For more information
contact South-Western,
5191 Natorp Boulevard,
Mason, Ohio 45040.
Or you can visit our Internet site at:
http://www.swlearning.com

Contents

1
The Scope of Corporate Finance

Chapter Summary

- The practice of corporate finance involves five functions: financing, capital budgeting, financial management, corporate governance, and risk management.

- The three legal forms of business organization are sole proprietorships, partnerships, and corporations. The new fourth form, the limited liability company, has become popular because of its favorable tax treatment and limited liability status.

- The goal of corporate financial managers is to maximize shareholder wealth, which implies that the managers must also satisfy customers, employees, suppliers, creditors, and other stakeholders first.

- Agency costs arise from the likelihood that managers may place personal goals ahead of corporate goals. Agency costs can be reduced by relying on market forces to exert managerial discipline, incurring monitoring costs to supervise managers, and structuring executive compensation contracts that align interests of managers and stockholders.

True or False Questions

T   F   1.   When a corporation sells securities to investors in exchange for cash, it raises capital in a secondary market transaction.

T   F   2.   Most stock market transactions and a large fraction of all bond market transactions involve secondary market trades.

T   F   3.   The United States represents about one-quarter of the world GDP and one-eighth of the total value of world trade.

T   F   4.   The capital structure decision is the single most important issue for a firm's financial managers.

T   F   5.   Market-driven risks relating to interest rates, commodity prices, and currency values are easily insurable.

T   F   6.   The most common form of business organization is the corporation.

T   F   7.   Any limited partnership must have one or more general partners, each
                   of whom has unlimited personal liability.

T   F   8.   Shareholders vote at an annual meeting to elect the president (CEO)
                   and corporate managers.

T   F   9.   An S corporation allows shareholders to be taxed as partners while still
                   retaining their limited liability status as corporate shareholders.

T   F   10.   Modern finance asserts that the goal of the firm is to maximize profits.

Multiple Choice Questions

1.   Which of the following is not a basic corporate finance function?

       a.   Risk-management function
       b.   Capital budgeting function
       c.   Corporate governance function
       d.   Tax management function

2.   When a corporation sells securities in exchange for cash, it raises capital in a:

       a.   Primary market transaction.
       b.   Secondary market transaction.
       c.   Third market transaction.
       d.   Fourth market transaction.

3.   In the 1990-2001 period, the share of U.S. issuers relative to the total value of
       securities issued by corporations around the world is about:

       a.   A quarter.
       b.   Three-eighths.
       c.   One-half.
       d.   Two-thirds.

4.   Commercial paper issued by corporations is a debt instrument maturing in:

       a.   One month or less.
       b.   One year or less.
       c.   Seven years or less.
       d.   More than seven years.

5. Which of the following is not a derivative instrument?

   a. Futures
   b. Options
   c. Preferred stocks
   d. Swaps

6. Which of the following business organization forms has unlimited personal liability?

   a. Partnerships
   b. Limited liability companies
   c. Corporations
   d. S corporations

7. To be eligible for S corporation status, the number of shareholders must be:

   a. 40 or fewer
   b. 60 or fewer
   c. 75 or fewer
   d. 100 or fewer

8. Modern finance asserts that the goal of the firm is to maximize:

   a. Profits.
   b. Sales.
   c. Earnings per share.
   d. Shareholder wealth.

9. The highest-paid U.S. executive in 2001 received a total pay of about:

   a. $136 million.
   b. $150 million.
   c. $392 million.
   d. $706 million.

10. Costs arising from the likelihood that managers may place personal goals ahead of corporate goals are called:

    a. Agency problems.
    b. Business ethics.
    c. Bonding expenditures.
    d. Stakeholder costs.

Questions and Problems

1. What are the advantages and disadvantages of the corporation as a legal form of business organization?

2. How does maximizing shareholder wealth differ from maximizing profits?

3. Calculate the tax disadvantage to organizing a U.S. business as a corporation instead of as a partnership under the following conditions. Operating income (gross profit before tax) will be $200,000 per year under either organizational form, the effective corporate tax rate (federal and state) is 40 percent, and the average personal tax rate for the owners of business is 36 percent. Assume that the corporation will distribute all income as dividends.

4. The stock price of GE in $33. Its CEO is awarded the option to buy 150,000 shares of GE stock at $35 per share. If the CEO exercises the stock option, what is his profit if the GE stock price increases to $40.50?

5. Motorola stock price is currently $20.75. Motorola awards its CEO an option to purchase 400,000 shares at $25 per share. How much stock-based compensation will the CEO receive if the stock price increases to $24 per share?

6. UAL has a choice between two projects, A and B. Project B could push the firm, which currently has a share price of $10, into bankruptcy. If project A is accepted, the firm's stock price will increase by 10%. If project B is accepted, the firm's stock price will increase by 20%. The CEO of UAL, afraid of the possible consequences of bankruptcy, accepts project A. What is the agency cost associated the decision on a per-share basis?

7. Oracle awards its CEO a stock option to buy 600,000 shares of its stock at $40 a share at anytime he wishes for the next ten years. The current stock price is $38.

    a. Suppose the stock price increases to $45 during the year, and the CEO exercises the option. How much stock-based compensation does he receive?

    b. Suppose the index of all technology stocks increases 35% during the year. Does the CEO deserve to profit on his options? Discuss.

    c. Suggest a method to avoid paying the CEO the earnings on the option when the whole stock market drifts upward.

8. Procter and Gamble's stock price is $91. Its CEO, who receives a salary of $900,000, is awarded an option to by 350,000 shares of the stock at $100 per share.

a.   If the CEO exercises the option, what is his profit if the stock increases to
        $110?

b.   Instead of awarding the CEO with stock options, Procter and Gamble pays
        him a salary of $2 million a year regardless of the company's
        performance. Is this a good or bad management decision for
        stockholders?

c.   Would it be better for stockholders to allow the CEO to buy the stock at
        $75 regardless of the market price? How about $140?

Solutions
True or False Questions

1.	F		6.	F
2.	F		7.	T
3.	T		8.	F
4.	F		9.	T
5.	F		10.	F

Multiple Choice Questions

1.	D		6.	A
2.	A		7.	C
3.	D		8.	D
4.	B		9.	D
5.	C		10.	A

Questions and Problems

1.   The corporate organization form has several advantages:

   - Unlimited life
   - Limited liability
   - Separate contracting
   - Unlimited access to capital

   Corporations have a major disadvantage: the double taxation problem. Corporate income is taxed at both company and personal levels.*

2.   Maximizing shareholder wealth is better then maximizing profits because the latter focuses on the past (instead of the future), ignores the timing of profits, relies on accounting principles rather than future cash flows, and ignores risk. Shareholder wealth maximization is socially optimal because shareholders are residual claimants who profit only after all other claims are paid, and such a goal encourages investment even under inherently risky conditions.

3.

	Corporation	Partnership
Operational income	$ 200,000	$ 200,000
Corporate income tax (40%)	(80,000)	0
Net income	120,000	200,000
Cash dividends or distributions	120,000	200,000
Personal tax on owner income (36%)	(43,200)	(72,000)
After-tax disposable income	$ 76,800	$ 128,000

   Conducting the business as a partnership rather than as a corporation can save the firm owners 26 cents ([128,000 – 76,800] / 200,000) in tax on every dollar earned.

4. The profit that the CEO makes is:

    ($40.50 - $35) (150,000 shares) = $825,000.

5. The CEO of Motorola receives zero stock-based compensation because the stock price is below the exercise price of $25 per share.

6. The agency cost on a per-share basis is:

    (20%) ($10) – (10%) ($10) = $1.

7. a. The stock-based compensation the CEO of Oracle receives is:

    ($45 - $40) (600,000 shares) = $3,000,000.

    b. The CEO of Oracle does not deserve to profit on his options because Oracle stock increases less than the general index of all technology stocks does—thus Oracle underperforms relative to the market.

    c. The exercise price of the stock option should be adjusted upward to reflect the increase of the stock market (or the increase of the index of all technology stocks).

8. a. The profit that the CEO earns is:

    ($110 - $100) (350,000 shares) = $3,500,000.

    b. This is a bad arrangement for shareholders because the CEO receives no incentives to pursue the goal of maximizing shareholder wealth.

    c. If the exercise price of the option is very low, say $75, the CEO will almost certainly profit even if he makes no effort to raise the value of the firm. On the other hand, if the exercise price is too high, such as $140, the CEO may feel that it is impossible to raise the stock price to that level. Therefore, the CEO's incentive to make an effort to increase shareholder wealth will be very small.

* Under legislation currently being considered by Congress, corporate income taxes would be reduced or perhaps even eliminated entirely.

2

Financial Statement and Cash Flow Analysis

CHAPTER SUMMARY

- The four principal financial statements are the balance sheet, the income statement, the statement of retained earnings, and the statement of cash flows.

- To calculate the firm's cash flow from operations, depreciation and other non-cash changes are added to net profit after taxes. Financial managers are interested in the firm's free cash flow--the amount of cash flow available to investors. It is calculated by deducting the net investment in fixed and current assets from the operating cash flow.

- The statement of cash flows describes the firm's cash flows over a period of time. It divides cash flows into operating, investment, and financing flows.

- Managers use financial ratios to analyze the firm's financial statements. Financial ratios are divided into five categories: liquidity, activity, debt, profitability, and market ratios. The DuPont system breaks the return on total assets and the return on common equity into component pieces. This system emphasizes the influence of the net profit margin, total assets turnover, and financial leverage on a firm's profitability.

TRUE OR FALSE QUESTIONS

T F 1. Accountants generally construct financial statements using a cash flow approach.

T F 2. The Financial Accounting Standards Board (FASB) is responsible for regulating publicly traded companies.

T F 3. By definition, a firm's assets must be equal to the combined value of its liabilities and stockholders' equity.

T F 4. A balance sheet shows assets on the right-hand side and the claims of the creditors and shareholders on the left-hand side.

T F 5. The term "gross property, plant, and equipment" in the balance sheet represents the original cost of real property, structures, and long-lived equipment owned by the firm minus the accumulated depreciation.

T F 6. Deferred taxes represent an estimate of future income taxes payable as a result of the firm using a more aggressive method to depreciate assets for tax purposes than that used for financial reporting to shareholders.

T F 7. Empirical research suggests that firms have a target dividend payout ratio based on their current earnings.

T F 8. Operating flows are cash inflows and outflows directly related to the production and sale of firm's products or services.

T F 9. A decrease in an asset is an inflow of cash.

T   F 10. The DuPont system breaks the ROA and ROE ratios into component pieces, emphasizing the influence of the net profit margin, total asset turnover, and financial leverage on a firm's profitability.

MULTIPLE CHOICE QUESTIONS

1. Which of the following is not a key financial statements required by the SEC for reporting shareholders?

   a. The statement of cash flows
   b. Notes to financial statements
   c. The income statement
   d. The statement of retained earnings

2. Which of the following assets is not a current asset?

   a. Intangible assets
   b. Inventories
   c. Marketable securities
   d. Accounts receivable

3. Which of the following is the least liquid current liability?

   a. Notes payable
   b. Accounts payable
   c. Accrued expenses
   d. Short-term bank loans

4. Which of the following companies has the highest global market value of global brand name in 2001?

   a. IBM
   b. General Electric
   c. Nokia
   d. Coca-Cola

5. Which of the following is not included in a firm's statement of cash flows?

a. Free cash flow
b. Cash flow from operations
c. Cash flow from financing
d. Cash flow from investment

6. A measure of a firm's ability to meet its short-term obligations is the:

a. Average collection period
b. Debt-to-equity ratio
c. Times interest earned ratio
d. Quick ratio

7. Which of the following ratios is used in the DuPont system?

a. Market/book ratio
b. Asset-to-equity ratio
c. Price/earnings ratio
d. Gross profit margin

8. An example of activity ratios is the:

a. Times interest earned ratio
b. Average collection period
c. Return on investment
d. Market/book ratio

9. Liabilities are presented on the balance sheet in descending order of:

a. Size
b. Age
c. Liquidity
d. Profitability

10. Total corporate cash flow is increased by:

a. Stock repurchase
b. Cash dividend
c. Stock dividend
d. The issuance of additional stock

QUESTIONS AND PROBLEMS

1. How does each of the following activities affect the year-end cash holding? In your answer, simply say "increase", "decrease" or "does not change".

a. Bought Treasury notes

   b. Paid stock dividends
   c. Exchanged debt for stock
   d. Issued additional stock
   e. Repaid bank debt
   f. Bought a new computer, paying cash

2. Albertson's quick ratio is 0.9, its current ratio is 1.5, and its current liabilities are $60 million. What is the value of Albertson's inventory?

3. Arizona Tea has a cash balance at the beginning of the year of $230,000. The company issued $1 million worth of stock and $5 million worth of bonds during the year. Dividends paid to stockholders totaled $100,000 and the interest paid was $400,000. Cash collected sales was $110,000 and depreciation expense was $60,000. Arizona Tea also sold teacups and coffee mugs for $15,000. What is the ending cash balance of Arizona Tea?

4. Cisco has a debt equity ratio of 1.2 and total assets of $580 million. How much debt is Cisco showing on its balance sheet?

5. Classify each of the following items as an inflow (I) or an outflow(O) of cash, or as neither (N)

	Item	Change
a.	Net loss	-900
b.	Cash	+450
c.	Depreciation	+1,100
d.	Notes payable	-300
e.	Sale of bonds	+1,850
f.	Accruals	+200
g.	Accounts receivable	-700

6. Complete the balance sheet and sales information in the table that follows for Intel Corporation using the following financial data:

Debt ratio: 0.4
Quick ratio: 0.9
Total assets turnover: 2.1
Days sales outstanding: 20 days (Assume 360 days in a year)
Gross profit margin: 30%
Inventory turnover ratio: 4

Balance Sheet

Cash	_____	Accounts payable	_____
Accounts receivable	_____	Long-term debt	200,000
Inventories	_____	Common stock	_____
Fixed assets	_____	Retained earnings	380,000
		Total Liabilities and	
Total assets	900,000	Equity	_____
Sales	_____	Cost of goods sold	_____

7. Data for EDS and its industry averages follows:

EDS Company: Balance sheet as of December 31,2002.

Cash	$50,000	Accounts payable	$90,000
Accounts receivable	210,000	Notes payable	110,000
Inventories	180,000	Accrued expenses	120,000
Total current assets	440,000	Total current assets	370,000
Net fixed assets	230,000	Long-term debt	100,000
		Common equity	200,000
Total assets	$670,000	Total liabilities and equity	$670,000

EDS Company: Income Statement for the year ended December 31,2002

Sales	1,620,000
Cost of goods sold	1,347,000
Gross profit	273,000
Selling expenses	98,000
General and administrative expenses	67,000
Earnings before interest and taxes	$108,000
Interest expense	11,000
Earnings before taxes	97,000
Federal income taxes (35%)	33,950
Net income	$63,050

Financial Ratios	EDS	Industry Average
Current ratio	_____	1.8
Average collection period	_____	31 days
Inventory turnover	_____	7.9
Total assets turnover	_____	3.5

Profit margin in sales	_____	2.9%
Return on total assets	_____	10.1%
Return on equity	_____	20.4%
Debt ratio	_____	50%

a. Calculate the indicated ratio for EDS

b. Which specific ratios seem to be the most out of line in relation to the industry averages?

c. What are EDS's strengths and weaknesses as revealed by your analysis?

SOLUTIONS

TRUE OR FALSE QUESTIONS

1.	F	6.	T
2.	F	7.	F
3.	T	8.	T
4.	F	9.	T
5.	F	10	T

MULTIPLE CHOICE QUESTIONS

1.	b	6.	d
2.	a	7.	b
3.	c	8.	b
4.	d	9.	c
5.	a	10	d

QUESTIONS AND PROBLEMS

1. a. Decrease
   b. Does not change
   c. Does not change
   d. Increase
   e. Decrease

2. Current assets of Albertson are:
   CA/$60 million=1.5   CA=$90 million
   The inventory of Albertson is:
   ($90 million-inventory)/$60 million=0.9
   $90 million-inventory=$54 million
   Inventory=$90 million-54 million=$36 million

3. The ending cash balance of Arizona Tea is:
   $230,000+($1,000,000+$5,000,000)-($1,000,000+$400,000)+$110,000+$15,000
   = $5,885,000
   (Note: Appreciation is not included because it is not a cash flow.)

4. Debt/Equity=1.2, Debt=(1.2)(Equity)
   Debt+Equity=$580 million
   1.2 Equity+Equity=$580 million
   Therefore, Equity=$263,636,364
   Debt=$580 million-$263,636,364=$316,363,636

5. a. Outflow of $900
   b. Outflow of $450
   c. Inflow of $1,100
   d. Outflow of $300
   e. Inflow of $1,850
   f. Inflow of $200
   g. Outflow of $700

6. Total Debt=(0.4)(Total Assets)=(0.4)(900,000)=$360,000

Accounts Payable=Total Debt-Long Term Debt=360,000-200,000=$160,000

Common Stock=Total Liabilities and Equity-Total Debt-Retained Earnings
          =900,000-360,000-380,000=$160,000

Sales=(2.1)(Total Assets)=(2.1)(900,000)=$1,890,000

Inventory=Sales/4=1,890,000/4=$472,500

Accounts Receivable=(Sales/360)(Days sales outstanding)
          =(1,890,000/360)(20)=$105,000

Cash+Accounts Receivable=(0.9)(Accounts Payable)
Cash+105,000=(0.9)(160,000)
Cash=144,000-105,000=$39,000

Fixed Assets=900,000-(39,000+105,000+472,500)=$283,500

Cost of Goods Sold=(Sales)(1-0.3)=(1,890,000)(0.7)=$1,323,000

7. a. Current Ratio = $\dfrac{\text{Current Assets}}{\text{Current Liabilities}}$ = $\dfrac{440,000}{370,000}$ = 1.19

   DSO = $\dfrac{\text{Accounts Receivable}}{\text{Sales}/365}$ = $\dfrac{210,000}{(1,620,000)/365}$ = 47.3 days

   Inventory Turnover = $\dfrac{\text{Cost of Goods Sold}}{\text{Inventory}}$ = $\dfrac{1,347,000}{1,800,000}$ = 7.48

   Total Asset Turnover = $\dfrac{\text{Sales}}{\text{Total Assets}}$ = $\dfrac{1,620,000}{670,000}$ = 2.42

   Profit Margin on Sales = $\dfrac{\text{Net income}}{\text{Sales}}$ = $\dfrac{63,050}{1,620,000}$ = 3.89%

$$ROA = \frac{\text{Net income}}{\text{Total Assets}} = \frac{63{,}050}{670{,}000} = 9.41\%$$

$$ROE = \frac{\text{Net income}}{\text{Common Equity}} = \frac{63{,}050}{200{,}000} = 31.53\%$$

$$\text{Debt Ratio} = \frac{\text{Total Debt}}{\text{Total Assets}} = \frac{470{,}000}{670{,}000} = 70\%$$

b. The ratios that seem to be the most out of line with industry average are the current ratio, days sales outstanding, the ROE and the debt ratio.

c. EDS has a good profit margin on sales, decent inventory turnover and excellent ROE. However, the firm is not liquid (low current ratio), has a very high level of debt, and seems to have problems collecting receivables. Due to its collection problems, the total asset turnover is below the industry average.

3
PRESENT VALUE

CHAPTER SUMMARY

- This chapter presents the technique for calculating the future value of a lump sum, the future value of a mixed stream, and the future value of an annuity for a given interest rate. Using a financial calculator or a spreadsheet program can simplify these calculations.

- The counterpart of computing future value is determining the present value of a lump sum, a mixed stream, an annuity, or a perpetuity.

- The future value and present value techniques can be applied to find the values of other variables, such as cash flow, interest rate, and number of time periods.

- Special applications of time value include: (1) compounding more frequently than annually, (2) stated versus effective interest rates, (3) the calculation of deposits needed to accumulate a future sum, and (4) loan amortization

TRUE OR FALSE QUESTIONS

T F 1. Financial intermediaries eliminate the need for savers and borrowers to deal directly with each other. Instead, both parties need to deal only with intermediaries.

T F 2. Japan had the highest national savings rate among the major industrialized countries in 2001.

T F 3. The U.S personal savings rate was negative in 2001.

T F 4. Compound interest is interest paid only on the initial principal of an investment, not on the interest that accrues in earlier period.

T F 5. An annuity is a stream of equal cash flows paid at the end of every year forever.

T F 6. An ordinary annuity is an annuity for which payments occur at the beginning of each period.

T F 7. The future value of an annuity due is always greater than the future value of the comparable ordinary annuity.

T F 8. The more frequently interest compounds, the greater the amount of money that accumulates

T F 9. The effective annual rate is the stated annual rate found by multiplying periodic rate by the number of periods in one year.

T F10. Loan amortization refers to a situation in which a borrower makes equal periodic payments over time and a balloon payment at the end to fully repay a loan.

MULTIPLE CHOICE QUESTIONS

1. The equilibrium interest rate is the rate:

   a. set by the Federal Reserve
   b. that equates total savings and investment within an economy
   c. that major commercial banks borrow from one another.
   d. that large corporations pay when they borrow from commercial banks

2. Which of the following countries had the highest national savings rate in 2001?

   a. Italy
   b. Japan
   c. Belgium
   d. France

3. Which of the following countries had the lowest national savings rate in 2001?

   a. Sweden
   b. Canada
   c. United States
   d. Australia

4. The separation of investment and financing decision rule means that:

   a. Corporations should accept all positive net present value projects, regardless of which investors are financing these projects
   b. Corporations must satisfy personal preferences of investors when making investment decisions
   c. Investment decisions and financing decisions must be made by two different corporate managers
   d. Investment decisions are separated and less important than financing decisions

5. A deposit made in an account paying 20% interest compounded annually over a 20-year period is worth approximately ....as the same amount deposited in an account earning only 10% interest compounded annually over the same period.

    a. one and a half times
    b. twice
    c. three times
    d. four times

6. The simplest modern example of a perpetuity is a:

    a. Preferred stock
    b. Treasury bond
    c. Mortgage
    d. Dividend-paying common stock

7. For a given interest rate, the future value of an investment is highest when interest rate is compounded:

    a. daily.
    b. annually.
    c. monthly.
    d. continuously.

8. A credit card that charges 1.5 percent per month has an effective annual rate of:

    a. 18 percent.
    b. 19.56 percent.
    c. 20.11 percent.
    d. 23.14 percent.

9. The variables you must know to amortize a loan include:

    a. The frequency of periodic payments
    b. The interest rate
    c. The total amount of the loan
    d. The term (length of the loan)
    e. b and c only
    f. a, b and c only
    g. b, c and d only
    h. a, b, c and d

10. The equal annual end-of-year deposits required to accumulate $100,000 at the end of five years, given an interest rate of 6 percent is:

    a. $17,740.88

    b. $18,805.33
    c. $17,921.44
    d. $20,000

QUESTIONS AND PROBLEMS

1. Would you prefer $1,000 now or $1,500 five years from now? The interest rate is 8%.

2. A winning lottery ticket pays you $50,000 a year for the next 20 years. The first payment is made today. If the discount rate is 9%, how much is that lottery ticket worth today?

3. You want to save money for your retirement 10 years from now by depositing money in your IRA.

    a. How much money do you have at retirement if you deposit $1,500 each 6 months for ten years at an interest rate of 12% compounded semi-annually?

    b. How much money do you have at retirement if you deposit $750 each 3 months for ten years at an interest rate of 12% compounded quarterly?

    c. Why do you have more money in part (b) than part (a)?

4. Cecilia has just purchased a new Toyota Camry for $22,000. If she makes a $2,000 down payment on the new car, what is her monthly payment to the bank that charges 12% per year for a 24-month car loan?

5. To supplement her educational expenses, Christine has obtained a part-time job. Her new employer estimates her gross pay for the next four years to be $5,000, $5,500, $6,100, and $6,900. What is the present value of the future earnings if they are discounted at 7%?

6. Suppose you have just won the lottery: $100,000 a year for 20 years. The first payment is made one year from now.

    a. If you deposit $100,000 each year into an account earning 8%, how much do you have at the end of 12 years?
    b. If your discount rate is 10%, how much is your winning lottery ticket worth today?
    c. How does your answer to part (b) change if you receive $50,000 every six month for 20 years?

7. Mrs. Jones bought 100 shares of General Electric in March 1993 for $34 a share. She sold all the shares in March 2000 for $5,110. What is the annual rate of return?

8. Suppose you borrow a certain sum of money from your college at an interest rate of 8%. Which of the repayment schedule would you prefer?

    a. You pay $20,000 in exactly one year
    b. You pay $11,000 in one year and an additional $10,000 in two years
    c. You pay $7,500 per year at the end of each of the next three years

9. Joseph Truman is shopping around for the best interest rates for his investment in a certificate of deposit over the next year. He has found the following at three different banks:

	Stated Rate	Compounding
Bank One	5.10%	Annually
LaSalle Bank	5.00%	Semiannually
Bank of America	4.80%	Quarterly

    a. Which bank offers Joseph the highest effective rate of return?
    b. Joseph decides to invest his money for only six months and the annual compounded rate of 5.1% is not available. Which of the remaining banks should Joseph choose?

10. Ann Kennedy borrowed $10,000 at a 6% annual interest rate to be repaid over three years. The loan is amortized into three equal annual end-of-year payments.

    a. What is the annual end-of-year loan payment that Ann must make?
    b. Prepare a loan amortization schedule for Ann
    c. Why does the interest portion of each payment decline each year?

SOLUTIONS

TRUE AND FALSE QUESTIONS

1.	T		6.	F
2.	F		7.	T
3.	T		8.	T
4.	F		9.	F
5.	F		10.	F

MULTIPLE CHOICE QUESTIONS

1.	b		6.	a
2.	d		7.	d
3.	c		8.	b
4.	a		9.	d
5.	c		10.	a

QUESTIONS AND PROBLEMS

1. I prefer $1,500 five years from now because its present value is: $1,500 / $(1.08)^5$ = (1,500) (0.6808) = $1,020.90.

2. The winning lottery ticket is worth:

   PV (annuity due) = $\dfrac{PMT}{r}$ x [1 - $1/(1+r)^n$] x (1+r)

   $$= \dfrac{50{,}000}{0.09} \text{ x } [\ 1 - 1/(1.09)^{20}]\ (1.09)$$

   $$= \dfrac{50{,}000}{0.09} \text{ x } (1 - 1/5.6044)\ (1.09)$$

   $$= \dfrac{50{,}000}{0.09} \text{ x } 0.8955 = \$497{,}500$$

Alternatively, you can use the present value factor for annuities to find the value of the winning lottery ticket:

PV=$50,000 (PVFA $_{9\%,20}$) (1.09) = 50,000 (9.1285) (1.09) = $497,503.

3. a. At retirement, you will have:
    $1,500 (FVFA $_{6\%,\,20}$) – 1,500 (36.786) = $55,179.

    b. If interest is compounded quarterly, you will have:
    $750 (FVFA $_{3\%,\,40}$) = 750 (75.401) = $56,550.75.

    c. When interest is compounded quarterly instead of semi-annually, you can earn a
       higher effective interest rate and have more money for retirement.

4. The amount that Cecilia has to finance is:
    $22,000 - $2,000 = $20,000
    The monthly statement is 12% / 12 months = 1%
    The monthly payment is:
    $20,000 / PVFA $_{1\%,\,24}$ = $20,000 / 21.2434 = $941.47.

5. The present value of Christine's future earnings is:
    $5,000 (PVFA $_{7\%,\,1}$) + $5,500 (PVFA $_{7\%,\,2}$) +$6,100 (PVFA $_{7\%,\,3}$) + $6,900
    (PVFA $_{7\%,\,4}$)
    = 5,000(0.9346) + 5,500(0.8734) + 6,100(0.8163) + 6,900(0.7629)
    = 4,673 + 4,803.70 + 4,979.43 + 5,264.01 = $19,720.14.

6. a. At the end of 12 years, you will have:
    $100,000 (FVFA $_{8\%,\,12}$) = $100,000 (18.977) = $1,897,700
    b. Your winning lottery ticket is worth;
    $100,000 (PVFA $_{10\%,\,20}$) = $100,000 (8.5136) = $851,360
    c. If you receive $50,000 every six months for 20 years, your winning lottery is
    worth:
    $50,000 (PVFA $_{5\%,\,40}$) = $50,000 (17.1591) = $857,955

7. $5,110 / $3,400 = 1.503
    Using the future value table, if we look across the table for a factor close to 1.503
    where n = 7 years, we find the annual rate of return to be 6%.

8. a. $20,000 / 1.08 = $18,518.52
    b. ($11,000 / 1.08) + $10,000 (1.08)^2 = $18,785.19
    c. ($7,500) (PVFA $_{8\%,\,3}$) = $7,500 (2.5771) = $19,328.25
    I want to minimize my payment. Therefore, I choose to pay $20,000 in one year.

9. a. Bank One: EAR = 5.10%
       LaSalle Bank: EAR = $(1+ \underline{0.05} \ )^2 - 1 = 5.06\%$

2

Bank of America: $\text{EAR} = (1 + \dfrac{0.048}{4})^4 - 1 = 4.89\%$

Bank One offers the highest effective rate of return

b. Joseph should choose LaSalle Bank because it offers a higher effective rate of return.

10. a. The annual end-of-year payment is:
$\text{PMT} = \$10{,}000 / \text{PVFA}_{6\%,\,3} = \$10{,}000 / 2.673 = \$3{,}741.10$

b.

Year	Beginning Amount	Payment	Interest	Repayment of Principal	Remaining Balance
1	$10,000	$3,741.10	$600.00	$3,141.10	$6,858.90
2	6,858.90	3,741.10	411.50	3,329.60	3,529.30
3	3,529.3	3,741.10	211.80	3.529.30	0
		$11,223.30	$1,223.30	$10,000	

c. The interest portion of each payment declines each year because the outstanding balance of the loan decreases.

4

BOND and STOCK VALUATION

CHAPTER SUMMARY

- The value of a bond, a stock, or any security is the present value of the cash flows that will accrue to a security holder over that security's life. The discount rate used to value a security is based on the risk of that security's cash flows. U.S. Treasury securities are discounted at a risk-free rate. Other debt and equity securities are discounted at a higher rate to reflect their default risk.

- Bond prices move in the opposite direction of market interest rates, and prices of long-term bonds are more sensitive to interest rate changes than are prices of short-term bonds.

- The term structure of interest rates describes the relation between time to maturity and yield to maturity on bonds with similar risk. The yield curve is the graphic representation of the term structure of interest rates.

- Preferred s tock p ays a fixed p eriodic d ividend a nd h as n o fixed m aturity. A p referred stock can be valued using the formula for the present value of a perpetuity.

- Common stock is difficult to value because of the difficulty of estimating future dividends and the difficulty of determining an appropriate discount rate.

- Common stock valuation is simple when dividends are not growing or are growing at a constant rate. Valuation can become complex when the growth rate of dividends changes over time.

- Other approaches to valuing common stock include the free cash flow approach, the book value method, the liquidation value method, the Price/Earnings ratio, and the Price/Sales multiples method.

TRUE or FALSE QUESTIONS

T F 1. The greater the uncertainty about a security's future cash flows, the lower the discount rate investors will apply when discounting those cash flows to the present

T F 2. Generally, the coupon rate of a bond will fluctuate according to market conditions.

T F 3. A call feature of a bond allows bondholders to redeem the bond at a predetermined price prior to maturity.

T   F 4. The bond equivalent yield is a simple interest measure of an investor's annual return from holding a Treasury bill.

T   F 5. The liquidity preference theory claims that investors should expect to earn the same return whether they invest in long-term Treasury bonds or a series of short-term Treasury bonds.

T   F 6. Corporations can exclude 70% of preferred dividend income from corporate tax.

T   F 7. Preferred stock has been in a decline for at least six decades and now represents under 5% of the net external financing for U.S. companies each year.

T   F 8. The constant growth model provides a useful way to frame stock valuation problems and can be applied to all types of firms, including those with very rapid growth.

T   F 9. Of more than 5,000 U.S. companies listed on the NYSE, AMEX and Nasdaq, as many as 70% pay no cash dividends in a given year.

T   F 10. The free-cash-flow approach offers an alternative to the dividend discount model that is especially useful when valuing shares that pay no dividends.

MULTIPLE CHOICE QUESTIONS

1. A call feature of a bond allows:

   a. Bondholders to redeem the bond at a predetermined price prior to maturity.
   b. Bondholders to redeem the bond at a predetermined number of shares in the borrowing firm.
   c. The issuer to redeem the bond at a predetermined price prior to maturity.
   d. The issuer to exchange the bond for a newly issued bond with lower coupon rate.

2. The annual coupon interest divided by the current market value of a bond is called the:

   a. Coupon rate
   b. Current yield
   c. Bond equivalent yield
   d. Yield to maturity

3. An example of a pure discount instruments is a:

   a. Treasury bill
   b. Treasury note
   c. Treasury bond
   d. Preferred stock

4. U.S government bonds are exposed to:

   a. default risk.
   b. foreign exchange risk.
   c. bankruptcy risk.
   d. interest rate risk.

5. Which of the following statements about preferred stock is false?

   a. Preferred stocks usually pay investors a fixed cash flow stream over time.
   b. Preferred stocks generally do not carry the right to vote.
   c. Preferred stocks face a tax disadvantage relative to bonds at the corporate level, and a capital gain disadvantage relative to common stocks at the investor level.
   d. Preferred stocks now represent under 3% of the net external financing for U.S. companies each year.

6. Of all the relatively simple stock valuation models, the model most used in practice is the:

   a. constant growth model.
   b. variable growth model.
   c. zero growth model.
   d. free cash flow model.

7. The percentage of the U.S. firms paying cash dividends in 1999 is approximately:

   a. 10%.
   b. 20%.
   c. 25%.
   d. 30%.

8. Which of the following common stock valuation methods uses historic accounting values?

   a. The price/earnings method
   b. The free cash flow method
   c. The price/sales method
   d. The liquidation value method

9. Which of the following statements about common stock valuation is false?

    a. Common stock is often very difficult to value because of the difficulty of estimating dividends far into the future.
    b. Discounting dividends to determine the stock price works well for stocks that pay dividends as well as for firms that have no history of paying dividends.
    c. Common stock valuation is much easier when dividends-per-share are growing at a constant rate.
    d. Both the book value and liquidation value approaches use historic accounting values rather than future cash flows.

10. The preferred habitat theory states that:

    a. the slope of the yield curve is influenced by only expected interest rate change.
    b. the slope of the yield curve is influenced not only expected interest rate changes, but also by the liquidity premium that investors require on long term bonds.
    c. when the yield curve is upward sloping, then investors must expect short term yields to rise.
    d. certain institutional investors have a strong desire to invest in long-term bonds to match their liabilities, even if long-term bonds offer low expected returns relative to a series of short-term bonds.

QUESTIONS and PROBLEMS

1. Suppose you wish to hold a 20-year bond for one year. The current price is $1,000 and a coupon of $70 is paid at the end of each year. The yield to maturity is 7%. Immediately after you buy the bond, the yield to maturity rises to 8%. What is your profit or loss in percent of the bond?

2. MCI issues a 30-year bond that pays an annual coupon $90 and has a face value of $1,000. The appropriate discount rate is 10%. What is the price of the bond?

3. A Tyco International bond is priced at $920. It will mature in ten years and has a face value of $1,000. The yield to maturity is 9%, and a coupon is paid at the end of each year. What is the value of the bond's coupon?

4. You have both a zero-coupon bond and a level coupon bond paying an annual coupon of $80. Both have 10 years left to maturity, a face value of $1,000, and a yield to maturity of 9%.

    a. Estimate each bond's current market price.

    b. Assume the yield to maturity increases to 10%. Determine the new marketprices and the percentage capital loss on each of these two bonds.

    c. Due to the decrease in the discount rate announced by the Federal Reserve, the yields to maturity of both bonds decrease from 9% to 7%. Determine the new market prices and the percentage capital gain (or loss) on each of these two bonds.

5. Dana Corporation is expected to pay a dividend of $1.60 at the end of the year. Based on the riskiness of this stock, you require a return of 13% and expect that the long-term growth rate for dividends of this company will be 8%. What is the stock price of Dana?

6. Kaman's current dividend is $2. The dividend is expected to increase at a rate of 6% indefinitely. You believe that the discount rate should be 10%. How much would you pay for this stock?

7. Ford Motors just declared a dividend of $0.50 per share for the most recent quarter, bringing to $2 its yearly dividend payment. They report a growth rate of 8% over the past ten years, a rate that you believe will hold over the long run. The appropriate discount rate for Ford is 12%.

    a. Based on this information, how much would you pay for the Ford stock?

    b. Ford stock is currently trading for $45 per share. What is the estimated growth rate?

    c. Ford suffers financial distress, the dividend is maintained at $2, but the stock price decreases to $34 per share. What is the growth rate?

SOLUTIONS

TRUE or FALSE QUESTIONS

1	F	6	F
2	F	7	T
3	F	8	F
4	T	9	F
5	F	10	T

MULTIPLE CHOICE QUESTIONS

1	c	6	a
2	b	7	b
3	a	8	d
4	d	9	b
5	d	10	d

QUESTIONS and PROBLEMS

1. The new price of the bond is:
$P = \$70 \ (PVFA_{8\%,20}) + \$1,000 \ (PVF_{8\%,20})$
$= \$70 \ (9.8181) + \$1,000 \ (0.2145) = 687.27 + 214.50 = \$901.77.$
The loss in percent of the bond is:
$(\$901.77 - \$1,000) \ / \ \$1,000 = -9.82\%.$

2. The price of the MCI bond is:
$P = \$90 \ (PVFA_{9\%,30}) + \$1,000 \ (PVF_{9\%,30})$
$= \$90 \ (9.4269) + \$1,000 \ (0.0573) = 848.42 + 52.3 = \$905.72.$

3. The value of the bond's coupon is:
$\$920 = C \ (PVFA_{9\%,10}) + \$1,000 \ (PVF_{9\%,10})$
$= C \ (6.4177) + \$1,000 \ (0.4224)$
$6.4177 \ C = 920 - 422.40 = \$497.60$
$C = \$77.54.$

4. a. The zero coupon bond's price is:
$P = \$1,000 \ / \ (1.09)^{10} = \$1,000 \ / \ 2.3674 = \$422.40.$

The level coupon bond's price is:
$P = \$80 \ (PVFA_{9\%,10}) + \$1,000 \ (PVF_{9\%,10})$
$= \$80 \ (6.4177) + \$1,000 \ (0.4224) = 513.42 + 422.40 = \$935.82.$

b. The new price of the zero coupon bond is:
$P = \$1{,}000 / (1.1)^{10} = \$1{,}000 / 2.5937 = \$385.55.$

The percentage capital loss for the zero coupon bond is:
$(\$385.55 - \$422.40) / \$422.40 = -8.72\%.$

The new price of the level coupon bond is:
$P = \$80 \, (PVFA_{10\%,10}) + \$1{,}000 \, (PVF_{10\%,10})$
$= \$80 \, (6.1446) + \$1{,}000 \, (0.3855) = 491.57 + 385.50 = \$877.07.$

The percentage capital loss for the level coupon bond is:
$(\$877.07 - \$935.82) / \$935.82 = -6.28\%.$

c. When the yield drops to 7%, the price of the zero-coupon bond is:
$P = \$1{,}000 / (1.07)^{10} = \$1{,}000 / 1.9672 = \$508.34.$

The percentage capital gain for the zero coupon bond is:
$(\$508.34 - \$422.40) / \$422.40 = 20.35\%.$

The level coupon bond's price is:
$P = \$80 \, (PVFA_{7\%,10}) + \$1{,}000 \, (PVF_{7\%,10})$
$= \$80 \, (7.0236) + \$1{,}000 \, (0.5083) = 561.89 + 508.30 = \$1{,}070.19.$

The percentage capital gain for the level coupon bond is:
$(\$1{,}070.19 - \$935.82) / \$935.82 = 14.36\%.$

5. The stock price of Dana Corporation is:
$P = D_1 / (k\text{-}g) = \$1.60 / (0.13 - 0.08) = \$32.$

6. The maximum price I would pay for Kaman stock is:
$P = D_0 \, (1+g) / (k\text{-}g) = \$2 \, (1.06) / (0.1 - 0.06) = \$53.$

7. a. The price of Ford Motors' stock is:
$P = D_0 \, (1+g) / (k\text{-}g) = \$92 \, (1.08) / (0.12 - 0.08) = \$54.$

b. Ford's estimated growth rate is:
$\$45 = \$2.16 / 0.12 - g)$
$g = 0.12 - (2.16 / 45) = 7.2\%.$

c. The new growth rate is:
$g = 0.12 - (2.16 / 34) = 5.6\%.$

5

RISK AND RETURN

Chapter Summary

- Risk is defined as the chance of financial loss. More sophisticated formulations define risk as variability of return or contribution to the variability of return of a portfolio.

- Most investors are assumed to be risk-averse, requiring compensation for taking risk. A risk-neutral person prefers investment with higher returns whether or not they have greater risk. A risk-seeking investor prefers to take risk even when the expected return on an investment falls below zero.

- There are several measures of risk: variance, standard deviation, covariance, correlation, and systematic risk (Beta).

- There is a risk-return tradeoff. If investors want higher expected returns on an investment, they must accept higher risks.

- When a security is part of a well-diversified portfolio, only the systematic risk of that security affects the expected return.

True or False Questions

T   F   1. During the past 30 years, the percentage of U.S. households that own common stock has more than doubled to 70 percent.

T   F   2. Common stock is the most junior financial claim.

T   F   3. During the twentieth century, the equity premium in the United States averaged 5.7 percent.

T   F   4. A risk-seeking investor prefers investments with higher returns, whether or not they have greater risk.

T   F   5. If returns vary through time, the geometric average will always fall below the arithmetic mean.

T   F   6. A portfolio generally exhibits less volatility than its individual stocks.

T   F   7. The covariance ranges between a maximum value of 1.0 and a minimum value of −1.0.

T   F   8. Because unsystematic risk can be eliminated through diversification, the market does not reward investors for bearing unsystematic risk.

T   F   9. A stock's beta can only be positive.

T   F   10. The beta of a stock equals the covariance of the stock's return with the returns on the market portfolio divided by the market portfolio's variance.

Multiple-Choice Questions

1. Which of the following countries has the lowest percentage of stock ownership by households?

   a.   Japan
   b.   United States
   c.   Australia
   d.   Sweden

2. Which of the following statements about common stock is false?

   a.   Common stock is the most junior financial claim.
   b.   Common stock has a history of great variability.
   c.   Common stock offers an uncertain stream of cash dividend payments.
   d.   Common stock promises a fixed, legally enforceable return.

3. During the past 30 years, the percentage of U.S. households that own common stock, either directly as part of their investment portfolio or indirectly as part of their pension fun, has more than doubled to:

   a.   40 percent.
   b.   50 percent.
   c.   60 percent.
   d.   70 percent.

4. The equity risk premium is the difference in annual returns between:

   a.   Common stocks and Treasury bills.
   b.   Common stocks and Treasury bonds.
   c.   Common stocks and preferred stocks.
   d.   Preferred stocks and Treasury bills.

5. Using a 20-year holding period, common stocks have:

    a.   A lower standard deviation than either Treasury bonds or bills.
    b.   Approximately the same standard deviation as Treasury bonds or bills.
    c.   A standard deviation twice as large as that of Treasury bills.
    d.   A standard deviation three times as large as that of Treasury bills.

6.   Which of the following statements about risk aversion is false?

    a.   Risk-averse investors will not accept a fair bet.
    b.   Risk-seeking investors prefer to take risk but will not accept investments whose expected returns fall below zero.
    c.   Risk-neutral investors prefer investments with higher returns whether or not they entail greater risk.
    d.   Risk-averse investors require compensation for taking risk.

7.   In a two-stock portfolio, risk reductions is maximized when the correlation coefficient of two stocks is:

    a.   +1.0.
    b.   0.0.
    c.   +0.4.
    d.   −1.0.

8.   Which of the following does not affect the variance of a portfolio of stocks?

    a.   Variances of individual stocks.
    b.   Weights of individual stocks.
    c.   Expected returns of individual stocks.
    d.   Covariances of pairs of stocks.

9.   As the number of stocks in the portfolio becomes very large:

    a.   The average variance of individual stocks has no impact on the portfolio variance.
    b.   The portfolio variance becomes the weighted average of the variances of individual stocks.
    c.   The expected return of the portfolio tends to decrease.
    d.   The portfolio variance falls below the average covariance of stocks in the portfolio.

10.   The beta of a common stock:

    a.   Cannot be negative.

    b.   Equals the covariance of the stock's return with the returns on the market portfolio divided by the portfolio's standard deviation.

    c.   Equals the covariance of the stock's returns with the returns on the market portfolio divided by the portfolio's variance.

    d.   Equals the covariance of the stock's returns with the returns on the market portfolio divided by the portfolio's expected returns.

Questions and Problems

1.   Suppose you invest 30% of your wealth in General Electric with a 15% standard deviation and the remainder of your wealth with 3M with a standard deviation of 20%. The correlation coefficient of these two stocks is 0.5. What is the standard deviation of your portfolio?

2.   Given the following probability distribution, calculate the expected return and the standard deviation of returns for GM.

State of the Economy	Probability	GM's Rate of Return
Boom	0.2	30%
Normal	0.6	15%
Recession	0.2	5%

3.   Calculate the standard deviation of the expected dollar returns for Wal-Mart, given the following distribution of returns.

Probability	Dollar Return
0.3	$40
0.6	$30
0.1	-$10

4.   The price of Procter and Gamble stock one year from now will be $100 with a probability of 60% or $70 with a probability of 40%. The current stock price is $73. The risk-free interest rate is 5%. Calculate the risk premium of the stock.

5.   Consider the following expected returns, standard deviations, and correlation coefficients for the stocks listed below.

Stock	E(R)	S.D.(R)		$\rho_{1,2}$	$\rho_{1,3}$	$\rho_{2,3}$
1. AT&T	10%	8%		0.7	0.4	0.5
2. Dell	20%	25%				
3. Ford	16%	20%				

a.   Calculate the expected return and the standard deviation of the portfolio if you put 40% of your money in Ford and the remainder in Dell.

b.   Calculate the expected return and the standard deviation of an equally-weighted portfolio of AT&T and Dell.

c.   Calculate the expected return and the standard deviation of an equally-weighted portfolio of the three stocks.

6.   Suppose you are given the following information regarding the rates of return (in percent) on three securities:

State of the Economy	Probability	T-Bond	SBC	Bank One
Expansion	0.2	6	30	20
Normal	0.6	6	15	10
Recession	0.2	6	-10	0

Calculate the expected return and standard deviation for each security as well as the covariance and correlation coefficient for each possible pair of securities.

7.   The rates of return on Honeywell stock and on the market portfolio, R_m, for four years were as follows:

Year	Honeywell	R_m
1	30%	20%
2	22%	30%
3	-10%	10%
4	6%	4%

a.   Calculate the average returns of Honeywell and the market.
b.   Calculate the variance of Honeywell and the market.
c.   Calculate the covariance between Honeywell and the market.
d.   Calculate the beta of Honeywell.

8.   Two stocks, Albertson and Safeway, have betas equal to 0.85. However, Albertson's standard deviation is 20% larger than the standard deviation of Safeway. Which stock is more risky? Explain.

9.   "The risk of a portfolio is the weighted average of the risk of the individual stocks in your portfolio." Do you agree with this statement? Explain.

10.   Investment in U.S. Treasury bills yields a 4% rate of return with certainty.
       Texas Instrument stock yields 10% with probability of 0.2 and 20% with
       probability of 0.8. What is the risk premium of Texas Instrument?

SOLUTIONS

True or False Answers

1.	F		6.	T
2.	T		7.	F
3.	F		8.	T
4.	F		9.	F
5.	T		10.	T

Multiple-Choice Answers

1.	A		6.	B
2.	D		7.	D
3.	B		8.	C
4.	A		9.	A
5.	B		10.	C

Questions and Problems

1.   The portfolio's variance is:

$$\sigma_p^2 = (0.3)^2(15)^2 + (0.7)^2(20)^2 + 2(0.3)(0.7)(0.5)(15)(20)$$
$$\sigma_p^2 = 20.25 + 196 + 63 = 279.25.$$

The portfolio's standard deviation is:

$$\sigma_p = (279.25)^{1/2} = 16.71\%.$$

2.   The expected return of GM is:

$$E(R) = (0.2)(30) + (0.6)(15) + (0.2)(5)$$
$$E(R) = 16\%.$$

The variance of returns for GM is:

$$\sigma^2 = (30\text{-}16)^2(0.2) + (15\text{-}16)^2(0.6) + (5\text{-}16)^2(0.2)$$
$$\sigma^2 = 39.2 + 0.6 + 24.2 = 64.$$

The standard deviation of returns for GM is:

$$\sigma = (64)^{1/2} = 8\%.$$

3.   The expected dollar return for Wal-Mart is:

$$(40)(0.3) + (30)(0.6) + (-10)(0.1) = 12 + 18 - 1 = \$29.$$

The variance of Wal-Mart is:

$$\sigma^2 = (40\text{-}29)^2(0.3) + (30\text{-}29)^2(0.6) + (-10\text{-}29)^2(0.1)$$
$$\sigma^2 = 36.3 + 0.6 + 152.1 = 189.$$

The standard deviation of the expected dollar return for Wal-Mart is:

$$\sigma = (189)^{1/2} = \$13.75.$$

4.   The expected stock price of Proctor and Gamble stock one year from now is:

$$(100)(0.6) + (70)(0.4) = 60 + 28 = \$88.$$

The expected return is:

$$(88\text{-}73) / 73 = 20.55\%.$$

The risk premium of the stock is the difference between the expected return and the return on the risk-free asset. Therefore:

$$\text{Risk premium} = 20.55\% - 5\% = 15.55\%.$$

5.   a. The expected return of the portfolio of Dell and Ford is:

$$E(R_p) = (16)(0.4) + (20)(0.6) = 6.4 + 12 = 18.4\%.$$

The variance of the portfolio is:

$$\sigma_p^2 = (0.4)2(20)2 + (0.6)2(25)2 + 2(0.4)(0.6)(0.5)(20)(25)$$
$$\sigma_p^2 = 64 + 225 + 120 = 409.$$

The standard deviation of the portfolio is:

$$\sigma_p = (409)^{1/2} = 20.22\%.$$

b. The expected return of the portfolio of AT&T and Dell is:

$$E(R_p) = (10)(0.5) + (20)(0.5) = 15\%.$$

The variance of the portfolio is:

$$\sigma_p^2 = (0.5)2(8)2 + (0.5)2(25)2 + 2(0.5)(0.5)(8)(25)$$
$$\sigma_p^2 = 16 + 156.25 + 70 = 242.25.$$

The standard deviation of the portfolio is:
$$\sigma_p = (242.25)^{1/2} = 15.56\%.$$

c. The expected return of the equally-weighted portfolio of the three stocks is:

$$E(R_p) = (10 + 20 + 16)/3 = 15.33\%.$$

The variance of the portfolio is:

$$\sigma_p^2 = (1/3)^2[(8)^2 + (25)^2 + (20)^2 + 2(0.7)(8)(25) + 2(0.4)(8)(20) + 2(0.5)(25)(25)]$$
$$\sigma_p^2 = (0.11)(64 + 625 + 400 + 280 + 128 + 500)$$
$$\sigma_p^2 = (0.11)(1997) = 219.67.$$

The standard deviation of the portfolio is:

$$\sigma_p = (219.67)^{1/2} = 14.82\%.$$

6.   The Treasury bond is a risk-free asset which has 6% expected return and 0 standard deviation. The expected return of SBC is:

$$E(R) = (30)(0.2) + (15)(0.6) + (-10)(0.2) = 6 + 9 - 2 = 13\%.$$

The variance of SBC is:

$$\sigma^2 = (30\text{-}13)^2(0.2) + (15\text{-}13)^2(0.6) + (-10\text{-}13)^2(0.2)$$
$$\sigma^2 = 57.8 + 2.4 + 105.8 = 166.$$

The standard deviation of SBC is:

$$\sigma = (166)^{1/2} = 12.88\%.$$

The expected return of Bank One is:

$$E(R) = (20)(0.2) + (10)(0.6) + (0)(0.2) = 4 + 6 + 0 = 10\%.$$

The variance of Bank One is:

$$\sigma^2 = (20\text{-}10)2(0.2) + (10\text{-}10)2(0.6) + (0\text{-}10)2(0.2)$$
$$\sigma^2 = 20 + 0 + 20 = 40.$$

The standard deviation of Bank One is:

$$\sigma = (40)^{1/2} = 6.32\%.$$

The Treasury bond has zero covariance and zero correlation with any risky security.

The covariance of SBC and Bank One is:

$$\sigma_{1,2} = (30\text{-}13)(20\text{-}10)(0.2) + (15\text{-}13)(10\text{-}10)(0.6) + (\text{-}10\text{-}13)(0\text{-}10)(0.2)$$
$$\sigma_{1,2} = 34 + 0 + 46 = 80.$$

The correlation coefficient between SBC and Bank One is:

$$\rho_{1,2} = 80/(12.88)(6.32) = 0.98.$$

7.   a.   The average rate of return of Honeywell is:

$$(30 + 22 - 10 + 6)/4 = 12\%.$$

b.   The variance of Honeywell is:

$$\sigma^2 = [(30\text{-}12)^2 + (22\text{-}12)^2 + (\text{-}10\text{-}12)^2 + (6\text{-}12)^2]/(4\text{-}1)$$
$$\sigma^2 = (324 + 100 + 484 + 36)/3 = 392/3 = 130.67.$$

c.   The covariance between Honeywell and the market is:

$$\sigma_{h,m} = [(30\text{-}12)(20\text{-}16) + (22\text{-}12)(30\text{-}16) + (\text{-}10\text{-}12)(10\text{-}16) + (6\text{-}12)(4\text{-}16)]/3$$
$$\sigma_{h,m} = [(18)(4) + (10)(14) + (\text{-}22)(\text{-}6) + (\text{-}6)(\text{-}12)]/3$$
$$\sigma_{h,m} = (72 + 140 + 132 + 72)/3 = 138.67.$$

d.   The beta of Honeywell is:

$$\beta = \text{cov} / \sigma_m^2 = 138.67/130.67 = 1.06.$$

8.   If your portfolio consists of one stock, then the standard deviation is the proper measure of risk, and Albertson is the more risky stock. However, if you are adding another stock to your well-diversified portfolio, beta is the proper measure of risk, and Albertson and Safeway are equally risky.

9.   The statement is wrong. The risk of the portfolio, which is measured by the portfolio's standard deviation, depends not only on the risk of individual stocks in the portfolio, but also on the correlations among the stocks.

10.   The expected return on Texas Instrument is:

$$E(R) = (10)(0.2) + (20)(0.8) = -2 + 16 = 14\%.$$

The risk premium of Texas Instrument is:

$$14 - 4 = 10\%.$$

6

RISK AND RETURN: THE CAPM AND BEYOND

Chapter Summary

- Investors are rewarded with higher returns for taking risk, but only for taking on systematic risk. Risk-averse investors should hold only efficient portfolios, which maximize expected returns for a given level of risk.

- If investors can borrow and lend at the risk-free rate, they can create a new efficient portfolio called the optimal risky portfolio. All investors will hold this portfolio and change the percentage investment in this portfolio and risk-free rate assets to obtain the level of risk that fits their individual preferences.

- Under certain conditions, the optimal risky portfolio becomes the market portfolio, which consists of all risky assets, with each asset weighted by its market value relative to the total market value of all assets.

- The CAPM states that the expected return on a specific asset equals the risk-free rate plus a premium that depends on the asset's beta, and the expected risk premium on the market portfolio. The beta measures the systematic risk of an asset.

- Earlier empirical tests supported the CAPM, but recent research suggests that the CAPM gives an incomplete explanation of why some assets earn higher expected returns that other assets do.

- Two alternatives to the CAPM are the Arbitrage Pricing Theory (APT) and the Fama – French Three Factor model. Neither has replaced the CAPM in practice.

True of False Questions

T F 1. Investments with below average levels of systematic risk have betas greater than 1.0.

T F 2. A portfolio is efficient if it offers the highest expected return among the group of portfolios with equal or less volatility.

T F 3. The actual return on a risk-free asset is always equal to its expected return.

T F 4. In the world of only risky assets, there is one unique market portfolio that is efficient and it dominates all other risky portfolios.

T F 5. To determine the composition of the optimal portfolio, we only need to know the expected return and standard deviation of every risky asset.

T   F 6. In practice, the market portfolio does not exist, but we can approximate it with a diversified portfolio such as the Dow Jones Industrial Average.

T   F 7. The security market line quantifies the relation between the expected return and standard deviation of portfolios consisting of the risk-free asset and the market portfolio.

T   F 8. On the average business day, 4% of NYSE stock and about 15% of Nasdaq stocks do not trade at all.

T   F 9. The CAPM asserts that no factor other than beta should be systematically related to expected returns.

T   F 10. Unlike the CAPM, which is a single-factor model, the APT states that asset returns are driven by a group of different factors.

Multiple Choice Questions

1. Which of the following efficient frontiers is the best for risk- averse investors?

    a. The efficient frontier that consists of domestic stocks.
    b. The efficient frontier including domestic and foreign assets.
    c. The efficient frontier including domestic stocks and bonds.
    d. The efficient frontier including domestic stocks, bonds, and real estate.

2. Which of the following portfolios on the capital market line has the highest expected return?

    a. A portfolio invested in 50% in the risk-free asset and 50% in the market portfolio.
    b. A portfolio invested only in the risk-free asset.
    c. A portfolio invested only in the market portfolio.
    d. A portfolio invested 10% in the risk-free asset and 90% in the market portfolio.

3. Which of the following statements about the market portfolio is false?

    a. In practice, the market portfolio does not exist.
    b. The market portfolio consists of every available asset, with each asset weighted by its market value relative to the total market value of all assets.
    c. Investors can approximate the market portfolio with a diversified portfolio of many assets, such as the Standard & Poor's 500 Stock Index.
    d. The standard deviation of the market portfolio is equal to 1.0.

4. All portfolio located on the capital market line are:

    a. efficient.
    b. aggressive.
    c. inefficient.
    d. defensive.

5. The CAPM claims that:

    a. an asset can be located above CML.
    b. all assets must be located on the SML.
    c. an asset can be located above the SML.
    d. all assets must be located on the CML.

6. The beta of Microsoft, an aggressive stock, is:

    a. 0.9.
    b. 1.0.
    c. -0.2.
    d. 1.1.

7. On the average day, the percentage of Nasdaq stocks that do not trade is about:

    a. 6%
    b. 10%
    c. 14%
    d. 17%

8. Which of the following statements about the empirical evidence on the CAPM is false?

    a. Even with the benefit of hindsight, the CAPM can explain no more than 60% of the cross-sectional variation in stock returns.
    b. The relation between beta and returns is unstable.
    c. The size of the firm and the firm's book-to-market value ratio do a much better job than beta explaining why some stocks earn higher returns than others.
    d. After controlling for the size and book-to-market effects, there is almost no relation between beta and returns

9. The arbitrage pricing theory was developed by:

    a. Eugene Fama
    b. William Shape
    c. Eugene Fama and Kenneth French
    d. Stephen Ross

10. Which of the following is not a leading alternative to the CAPM?

a. Arbitrage pricing theory
b. Brennan's model
c. Fama-French model
d. All of the above are alternatives to the CAPM

Questions and Problems

1. Two stocks are purchased for $60 each at the beginning of a year. The expected stock prices of GM and Home Depot at the end of the year are $69 and $72, respectively. The market is in equilibrium, and the risk-free interest rate is 4%. The market portfolio's average rate of return is 14%. Calculate the betas of GM and Home Depot.

2. You invest in General Dynamics, which has a beta of 1.1. The risk-free rate of interest is 5%, and the expected return on the market portfolio is 13%. Using the SML, calculate the expected return of General Dynamics.

3. You are evaluating the common stocks whose average returns and betas are given below:

Stocks	Average Return	Beta
Dell	13.4%	1.2
Intel	13.0%	1.1
Coors	11.3%	0.9
Kraft	11.2%	0.8
Comcast	14.0%	1.3
S&P 500 Index	12.0%	1.0
Treasury Bills	5.0%	0

a. According to the CAPM, which stocks are underpriced, overpriced, or correctly priced?
b. Which stocks are aggressive?
c. Calculate the expected return and the beta of the equally-weighted portfolio of the five stocks?

4. The expected return on IBM is 14%, and its standard deviation is 29%. The risk-free return is 3%. Calculate the expected return and standard deviation on the following portfolios:

Portfolio	% Invested in IBM	% Invested in Risk Free Asset
A	20	80
B	50	50
C	70	30
D	120	-20

5. The return on Walmart is 17%, and its beta is 1.15. The risk-free return is 3%, and the expected return on the market portfolio is 14%. Does Walmart lie on, above, or below the security market line?

6. Suppose you believe that three risk factors drive stock returns: unexpected changes in the inflation rate, unexpected shifts in GDP, and unexpected changes in overall business risk in the economy. The risk premium for bearing inflation risk is 3%, the risk premium for bearing GDP risk is 4%, and the risk premium for bearing business risk is 5%. Citigroup's fortunes are very sensitive to inflation, meaning that its inflation beta is 1.6. Its GDP beta is 0.8, and its business risk beta is 0.9. If the risk-free rate is 4 %, what is the expected return on Citigroup?

7. Suppose that the expected risk-premium on small stocks relative to large stocks is 7%, and the expected risk premium on low book-to-market stocks relative to high book-to-market stocks is 5%. Also assume that the expected risk premium on the overall stock market relative to the risk-free rate is 6%. Anheuser Busch has a market beta of 0.9, a size beta of 0.4, and a book-to-market beta of 0.5. If the risk-free rate is 3%, what is the expected return on this stock according to the Fama-French model?

8. If Boeing has a beta of 1.3 and the standard deviation of the market is 25%, what is the covariance between Boeing and the market?

9. The risk-free asset pays 4%, the market portfolio's expected return is 12%, and its standard deviation is 30%. What is the slope of the capital market line?

SOLUTIONS

True of False Questions

1	F	6	F
2	T	7	F
3	T	8	F
4	F	9	T
5	F	10	T

Multiple Choice Questions

1	b	6	d
2	c	7	b
3	d	8	a
4	a	9	d
5	c	10	b

Questions and Problems

1. The expected return of GM is:
    ($69 - $60) / $60 = 15%.
    The expected return of Home Depot is;
    ($72 - $60) / $60 = 20%.
    Using the SML equation we can find the beta of GM:
    $$15\% = 4 + (14-4)b$$
    $$b = (15-4)/10 = 1.1.$$
    The beta of Home Depot is:
    $$20\% = 4 + (14-4)b$$
    $$b = (20-4) / 10 = 1.6.$$

2. Using the SML, the expected return of General Dynamics is:
    $E(R) = 5 + (13-5)(1.1) = 13.8\%.$

3. a. Using the SML equation, we have:

    Dell: $E(R) = 5 + (12-5)(1.2) = 13.4\%.$
    Dell has an average rate of return of 13.4%. It is correctly priced.

    Intel: $E(R) = 5 + (12-5)(1.1) = 12.7\%.$
    Intel has an average rate of return of 13%. It is underpriced.

    Coors: $E(R) = 5 + (12-5)(0.9) = 11.3\%.$
    Coors has an average rate of return of 11.3%. It is correctly priced.

Kraft: E(R) = 5+ (12-5)(0.8) = 10.6%.
Kraft has an average rate of return of 11.2%. It is underpriced.

Comcast: E(R) = 5+ (12-5)(1.3) = 14.1%.
Comcast has an average rate of return of 14%. It is overpriced.

b. The aggressive stocks are Dell, Intel, and Comcast. They all have betas greater than 1.0.

c. The expected return of the portfolio is:
$E(R_p) = (13.4 + 13 + 11.3 + 11.2 + 14) / 5 = 12.58\%$.
The beta of the portfolio is:
Beta = (1.2 +1.1 +0.9 + 0.8 +1.3) / 5 = 1.06.

4. The expected return of portfolio A is:
$$E(R_A) = (14\%)(0.2) + (3\%)(0.8) = 5.2\%.$$
The standard deviation of portfolio A is:
$$\sigma(R_A) = (29\%)(0.2) = 5.8\%.$$
The expected return on portfolio B is:
$$E(R_B) = (14\%)(0.5) + (3\%)(0.5) = 8.5\%$$
The standard deviation of portfolio B is:
$$\sigma(R_B) = (29\%)(0.5) = 14.5\%.$$
The expected return on portfolio C is:
$$E(R_C) = (14\%)(0.7) + (3\%)(0.3) = 10.7\%.$$
The standard deviation of portfolio C is:
$$\sigma(R_C) = (29\%)(0.7) = 20.3\%.$$
The expected return on portfolio D is:
$$E(R_D) = (14\%)(1.2) + (3\%)(-0.2) = 15\%.$$
The standard deviation of portfolio A is:
$$\sigma(R_D) = (29\%)(1.2) = 34.8\%.$$

5. According to the CAPM, the expected return on Walmart is:

E(R) = 3 + (16-3)(1.15) = 17.95%.
Walmart lies below the SML because its return is below its expected return of 17.95%.

6. According to the APT, the expected return on Citigroup is:
E(R) = 4 + (1.6)(3) + (0.8)(4) + (0.9)(5) = 4 + 4.8 + 3.2 + 4.5
    = 16.5%.

7. According to the Fama–French model, the expected return on Anheuser Busch stock is:
E(R) = 3 + (0.9)(6) + (0.4)(7) + (0.5)(5) = 3+5.4+2.8+2.5
    = 13.7%.

8. The covariance between Boeing and the market is:
    $\text{Cov}(R_i, R_m) = (\beta)(\sigma_m^2) = (1.3)(25)^2 = 812.5.$

9. The slope of the capital market line is:
    $(12 - 4) / 30 = 0.266$

7
CAPITAL BUDGETING PROCESS AND TECHNIQUE

Chapter Summary

- The capital budgeting process includes identifying, analyzing, and selecting investment projects that will create shareholder value.

- Simple capital budgeting techniques include the payback period, discount payback period, and accounting rate of return. More sophisticated techniques include net present value (NPV), internal rate of return (IRR), and profitability index (PI). These techniques deal with the time value of money and often, but not always, give the same accept-reject decisions.

- In general, the NPV is the best capital budgeting technique.

True of False Questions

T   F   1. Capital spending refers to investments in long-lived assets.

T   F   2. The payback method is the simplest and most popular technique of all capital budgeting decision tools.

T   F   3. The payback method assigns a 0 percent discount rate to cash flows that occur before the cutoff point.

T   F   4. The accounting rate of return method makes no adjustment for project risk or for the time value of money.

T   F 5. A drawback to the NPV rule is that it does not incorporate the value of managerial flexibility when calculating a project's NPV.

T   F 6. The internal rate of return always yields investment recommendations that are in agreement with the NPV rule.

T   F 7. When projects have initial cash inflows and subsequent cash outflows, invest when the project IRR exceeds the hurdle rate.

T   F 8. When choosing between mutually exclusive investments, the one offering the highest IRR provides the greatest wealth-creation opportunity.

T   F 9. The decision rule to follow when evaluating investment projects using the profitability index is to invest when the PI is greater than 1.0.

T   F 10. Under capital rationing, ranking projects using the IRR will generate a higher NPV than any other ranking methods.

Multiple Choice Questions

1. Which of the following methods is a simple capital budgeting method?

   a. profitability index
   b. net present value
   c. internal rate of return
   d. discounted payback rule

2. Which of the following capital budgeting methods does not use the time value of money?

   a. discounted payback rule
   b. profitability index
   c. accounting rate of return
   d. internal rate of return

3. Which of the following statements about the payback methods is false?

   a. The payback cutoff period is an arbitrary choice with little connection to shareholder value maximization.
   b. The payback method assigns a 0 percent discount rate to cash flows that occur before the cutoff point.
   c. Managers who follow the payback rule tend to underinvest in long-term projects that could offer substantial reward for shareholders.
   d. The payback method gives a direct estimate of the change in shareholder wealth resulting from a given investment.

4. When the NPV and IRR rules produce conflicting investment decisions, the firm should:

   a. use the NPV rule.
   b. use the IRR rule.
   c. be indifferent between the IRR rule and NPV rule.
   d. use the profitability index.

5. One advantage of the NPV rule over the IRR rule is that the:

   a. precise cost of capital is not needed to calculate NPV.
   b. NPV rule is consistent with the firm's goal of maximizing stockholders' wealth.
   c. NPV rule is superior in dealing with independent projects.
   d. NPV, which is stated in dollar terms, is easier to compare with other statements.

6. A drawback of the accounting rate of return is that:

   a. the ARR rule does not discount income.
   b. the ARR rule can be used to supplement the IRR rule.
   c. the ARR rule discounts income at the cost of capital.
   d. the ARR rule cannot be used to rank mutually exclusive projects.

7. The internal rate of return is best explained by:

   a. the point where the initial investment is recovered.
   b. the reciprocal of the payback period.
   c. the rate which equates NPV to zero.
   d. the accounting rate of return.

8. Which of the following methods is rarely used by large, publicly traded firms?

   a. accounting rate of return
   b. NPV
   c. IRR
   d. payback method

9. Under capital rationing, which method should a firm use in ranking projects?

   a. NPV
   b. IRR
   c. profitability index
   d. payback method

10. Which of the following statements is false?

    a. The NPV rule considers the scale on magnitude of the initial investment.
    b. For mutually exclusive projects, the NPV and IRR rules lead to the same investment decisions.
    c. If the profitability index is greater than one, a firm should accept the project.
    d. The payback method ignores cash flows received after the payback period.

Questions and Problems

1. Suppose you are considering the following two mutually exclusive projects:

Year	0	1
Cash flows		
Project A	-$1,000	$1,500
Project B	-$10,000	$12,500

The cost of capital is 9%. Calculate the two projects' NPVs and IRRs. Which project is better according to the NPV rule? Which project is better according to the IRR rule?

2. Why do firms continue to use the payback period rule despite its serious deficiencies?

3. Calculate the payback period from the following cash flows:

Year	Cash flow A	Cash flow B
0	-$6,000	-$12,000
1	$1,000	$2,000
2	$2,000	$4,000
3	$3,500	$5,000
4	$1,000	$3,000
5	$2,000	$1,000

4. Suppose that you have two mutually exclusive projects with the following cash flows:

Year	0	1	2	3
Project X	-$5,000	$1,000	$2,000	$3,500
Project Y	-$9,000	$2,000	$6,000	$4,000

Assume the cost of capital is 9%, what is the profitability index for each project? Which project do you accept?

5. You are considering projects with the following cash flows:

Year	0	1	2	3
Project X	-$9,000	$4,000	$4,000	$4,000
Project Y	-$10,334	$3,000	$5,000	$6,000

What is the IRR for each project?

6. You are considering two mutually exclusive projects with the following cash flows:

Year	0	1	2	3	4
Project Y	-$8,000	$1,000	$3,000	$3,000	$4,000
Project Z	-$11,00	$4,000	$5,000	$2,000	$4,000

Assume the cost of capital is 10%, what is the NPV for each project? Which project do you accept?

7. A project has the following cash flows:

Year	0	1	2	3
Cash flows	-$110	$30	$40	$60

The cost of capital is 8% for the first year, 10% for the second year, and 14% for the third year. Calculate the project's NPV. Would you accept the project?

8. The CFO of GE is considering two mutually exclusive projects, A and B, with the following cash flows:

Expected Cash Flows

Year	Project A	Project B
0	-$500,000	-$500,000
1	200,000	$200,000
2	250,000	$250,000
3	300,000	$500,000

Both projects have a cost of capital of 10%.

a. What are the projects' payback periods?
b. Calculate two projects NPVs
c. What are the two projects' IRRs?
d. Calculate the profitability index for both projects
e. Which project should the CFO choose? Why?

9. You are a vice-president of finance at Prudential. You are considering two mutually exclusive projects. Project A has a cost of $100,000 and produces a cash flow of $35,000 per year for five years. Project B costs $300,000 and produces a net cash flow of $100,000 per year for five years. Calculate the two projects' NPVs, IRRs, and PIs, assuming a cost of capital of 10%. Which project would you select? Why?

Solutions

True of False Questions

1	T	6	F
2	F	7	F
3	T	8	F
4	T	9	T
5	T	10	F

Multiple Choice Questions

1	d	6	a
2	c	7	c
3	d	8	a
4	a	9	c
5	b	10	b

Questions and Problems

1. The NPV of project A is:
($1,500 / 1.09) - $1,000 = $376.15.

The NPV of project B is:
($12,500 / 1.09) - $10,000 = $1,476.89.

The IRR of project A is:
$1,500 / (1+r) = $1,000
1+r = $1,500 / $1,000 = 1.5
r = 50%.

The IRR of project B is:
$12,500 / (1+r) = $10,000
r = 25%.

According to the NPV rule, project B is better, but the IRR rule selects project A. The NPV rule is superior because it maximizes shareholder wealth.

2. Firms use the payback period rule when the annual cash flows are more or less constant over the years. In addition, if the project has a long economic life and the annual cash flows do not vary much across years, the payback period rule will yield a decision similar to the IRR rule, which is optimal for independent and conventional projects.

3. The payback period of cash flow A is 2.86 years:
($1,000 + $2,000 + $3,000 out of $3,500).
The payback period of cash flow of B is 3.33 years:
($2,000 + $4,000 + $5,000 + $1,000 out of $3,000).

4. The profitability index of project X is:
[$1,000 (0.9174) + $2,000 (0.8417) + $3,500 (0.7722)] / $5,000 = 1.06.

The profitability index of project Y is:
[$2,000 (0.9174) + $6,000 (0.8417) + $4,000 (0.7722)] / $9,000 = 1.11.

You should accept project Y because it has a higher profitability index.

5. Because the cash flows of Project A are constant, the project's NPV=0 if:

$4,000 x DAF $_{r\%,3}$ = $9,000.
or DAF $_{r\%,3}$ = $9,000 / $4,000 = 2.25.

Use the present value of an annuity table, look at the time corresponding to 3 years, and move to the right to the number 2.2459. Therefore, the IRR of project A is 16%.

For Project B, the IRR is the value of r that solves the following equations:

$$- \$10,344 + \frac{\$3,000}{(1+r)} + \frac{\$5,000}{(1+r)^2} + \frac{\$6,000}{(1+r)^3} = 0$$

At r = 15%
NPV = 3,000(0.8696) + 5,000(0.7561) + 6,000(0.6575) – 10,334
        = 2,608.80 + 3,780.50 + 3,945 – 10,334 = 0
The IRR of project B is 15%.

6. The NPV of project Y is:
            1,000(0.9091) + 3,000(0.8264) + 3,000(0.7513) + 4,000(0.683) – 8,000
            = 909.10 + 2,479.20 + 2,253.90 + 2,732 – 8,000 = $374.20.
      The NPV of project Z is:
            4,000(0.9091) + 5,000(0.8264) + 2,000(0.7513) + 4,000(0.683) – 11,000
            = 3,636.40 + 4,132 + 1,502.60 + 2,732 – 11,000 = $1,003.

You should accept project Z because it has a higher NPV.

7. The NPV of the project is:
$$\frac{\$30}{1.08} + \frac{\$40}{(1.08)(1.10)} + \frac{\$60}{(1.08)(1.10)(1.14)} - \$110$$
= 27.78 + 33.67+44.30 – 110 = -$4.25.

You should not accept this project because its NPV is negative.

8.   a. The pay back period of project X is 2.17 years
200,000 + 250,000+50,000 out of 300,000 = 500,000.

The payback period of project Y is 2.4 years.
100,000 + 200,000 + 200,000 out of 500,000 = 500,000.

b. The NPV of project X is:
200,000(0.9091) + 250,000(0.8264) + 300,000(0.7513) - 500,000
= 181,820 + 206,600 + 225,390 - 500,000 = $113,810.

The NPV of project Y is:
100,000 (0.9091) + 200,000 (0.8264) + 500,000 (0.7513) – 500,000
= 90,190 + 165,280 + 375,650 – 500,000 = $131,840.

c. To calculate two projects' IRRs, use the trial-and-error method. For project X, the IRR is the value of r that solves the following equation:

$$- \$500,000 + \frac{\$200,000}{(1+r)} + \frac{\$250,000}{(1+r)^2} + \frac{\$300,000}{(1+r)^3} = 0.$$

At r=20%
NPV = 200,000 (0.8333) + 250,000 (0.6944) + 300,000 (0.5785) – 500,000
      = $13,810.

The IRR of project X is about 21%.

For project Y, the IRR is the value that solves the following equation:

$$- \$500,000 + \frac{\$100,000}{(1+r)} + \frac{\$200,000}{(1+r)^2} + \frac{\$500,000}{(1+r)^3} = 0.$$

At r=20%
NPV = 100,000 (0.8333) + 200,000 (0.6944) + 500,000 (0.5785) – 500,000
      = $11,460.

The IRR of project Y is also about 21%.

d. The profitability index of project X is:
(181,820 + 206,600 + 225,390) / 500,000 = 1.23.

The profitability index of project Y is:
(90,190 + 165,280 + 375,650) / 500,000 = 1.26.

e. The CFO should choose project Y because it has higher NPV. The NPV rule is superior because it maximizes shareholder wealth.

9. The NPV of project A is:
(35,000) (3.7908) − 100,000 = $32,678.

The NPV of project B is:
(100,000) (3.7908) − 300,000 = $79,080.

The IRR of project A is about 22%.
$35,000 (DFA_{r\%,5}) = 100,000$
$(DFA_{r\%,5}) = 100,000/35,000 = 2.8571$
$r = 22\%$.

The IRR of project B is about 20%
$100,000 (DFA_{r\%,5}) = 300,000$
$(DFA_{r\%,5}) = 300,000/100,000 = 3.0$.
$r = 20\%$

The profitability index of project A is:
132,678 / 100,000 = 1.33.

The profitability index of project B is:
179,080 / 300,000 = 0.6.

You should accept project B because it has higher NPV.

8

CASH FLOW AND CAPITAL BUDGETING

Chapter Summary

- To find operating cash flow, calculate after-tax net income and add back any non-cash expenses.

- The costs of financing an investment, such as interest expense, should not be counted as part of a project's cash outflows.

- Only incremental costs associated with a project should be included in NPV analysis. Opportunity costs should be included in cash flow projections, but sunk costs are excluded.

- Discount nominal cash flows at a nominal discount rate, and real cash flows at a real rate.

- When evaluating alternative fixed asset purchases with unequal lives, determine the equivalent annual cost of each fixed asset and choose one that is least expensive.

- When analyzing capital budgeting projects, the analyst should consider human factors and make sure that the project makes sense.

True or False Questions

T   F 1. Financial managers should measure the after-tax cash flows of a given investment by using the firm's average tax rate.

T   F 2. For capital budgeting purposes, financial analysts focus on incremental cash inflows and outflows.

T   F 3. In the United States, firms can keep separate sets of books, one for tax purposes and one for financial reporting purposes, using different depreciation methods for each set.

T   F 4. An increase in net working capital represents a cash inflow.

T   F 5. For capital budgeting purposes, firms must consider the incremental cash outflows from existing product sales that are cannibalized by a newer product.

T   F 6. Sunk costs must be included in cash flow projections.

T   F   7. Discounting real cash flows at a real interest rate should yield the same NPV as discounting nominal cash flows at a nominal rate.

T   F   8. If firms project nominal cash flows, which increase over time due to inflation, and discount those cash flows using a real rate, then they will understate the project's NPV.

T   F   9. When evaluating alternative equipment purchases with unequal lives, the firm should choose the equipment with the highest equivalent annual cost.

T   F 10. When a firm operates at less than full capacity, then the cost of using the excess capacity is zero.

Multiple Choice Questions

1. Which of the following countries allows firms to keep separate sets of books, one for tax purposes and one for financial reporting purposes, using different depreciation methods for each set?

    a. Sweden
    b. Germany
    c. United Kingdom
    d. Japan

2. Which of the following costs should firms avoid including in cash flow projections?

    a. opportunity costs
    b. sunk costs
    c. costs of using excess capacity
    d. cannibalization costs

3. Analysts should measure all cash flows of a project on:

    a. a before-tax basis
    b. an after-tax basis using the firm's marginal tax rate
    c. an after-tax basis using the firm's average tax rate
    d. an after-tax basis using either the firm's marginal tax rate or average tax rate

4. Which of the following transactions represents a cash outflow?

    a. an increase in net working capital
    b. a decrease in inventory
    c. an increase in accounts payable
    d. a decrease in accounts receivable

5. In capital budgeting, the alternative use of an asset owned by a firm is called a(n):

    a. sunk cost.
    b. cannibalization cost.
    c. incremental cost.
    d. opportunity cost.

6. With accelerated depreciation:

    a. a firm can depreciate an asset more than the purchase price.
    b. the NPV of a project is unchanged.
    c. a firm pays low taxes in earlier years and more taxes in later years.
    d. a firm pays less taxes.

7. Which of the following should not be deducted from the project's cash flows?

    a. interest charges
    b. taxes
    c. cannibalization costs
    d. changes in net working capital

8. The depreciation permitted for tax purposes is generally:

    a. not tax deductible.
    b. greater than the purchase price of the asset.
    c. adjusted for the inflation rate.
    d. different from the depreciation used for financial reporting purposes.

9. In estimating the cost of a new project, the firm should include:

    a. interest charges.
    b. opportunity costs.
    c. sunk costs.
    d. both a and b.

10. Which of the following statements is false?

    a. Only the incremental costs associated with a project should be included in NPV analysis.
    b. Decreases in working capital represent cash inflows.
    c. The nominal interest rate does not account for inflation.
    d. If you use nominal cash flows, use the real cost of capital to calculate the project's NPV.

Questions and Problems

1. Zayre's annual revenue from sales is $1,000,000. Zayre obtains cash for 60% of its sales and sells 40% on credit for one year. The firm purchases goods for $600,000 a year, paying 50% in cash and 50% in credit for one year. Suppose Zayre makes sales and purchases in years 1,2, and 3. Calculate Zayre's annual cash flows.

2. You are considering buying a flat-screen television set for $3,000. You have this sum but decide you can wait for the TV set and deposit your money in a bank for two years at an annual interest rate of 9%. After two years, you realize that the same TV set will cost you $3,400. Suppose the prices of all goods increase at the same rate as the TV set.

    a. What is the annual inflation rate?
    b. What is the real annual interest rate?

The following data apply to the next six problems

Boeing is considering a project that costs $900,000. The project is depreciated evenly over those years. The cash revenue before deducting depreciation and taxes is $650,000 in cash of the three years. The tax rate is 35%.

3. What are the firm's annual after-tax earnings?

4. What are the firm's after tax annual cash flows?

5. If the cost of capital is 12%, should Boeing accept the project?

6. If Boeing is allowed to use accelerated depreciation, 50% of its assets are depreciated in year 1, 30% in year 2, and 20% in year 3, does the accelerated depreciation affect the firm's after tax earnings? Compute the earnings.

7. Does the accelerated depreciation affect the firm's after-tax cash flows? Compute the cash flows.

8. Does the accelerated depreciation affect the project's NPV?

9. Honda is considering producing a larger motorcycle model. The estimated costs and the net cash flows from this project are (in millions):

	1	2	3	4	5
Cash Flows	-$600	$100	$150	$200	$200

This project will create a side effect for Honda: an increase in demand for spare parts. The net cash flow from the incremental demand for spare parts is zero for years 1 and 2, $10 million in year 3, and $15 million in years 4 and 5. The cost of capital is 9%.

    a. What is the project's NPV? Should Honda accept the project?
    b. What is the project's NPV if Honda has to spend an additional $20 million on machinery in year to spare parts?

10. Merck is considering whether to invest in research and development of a new drug. The firm estimates there is a 30% chance of research and development failing (zero cash flow will occur) and a 70% chance of a new drug being produced that will generate the following cash flow (in millions):

Year	1	2	3	4	5
Cash Flows	-$90	-$110	$200	$200	$100

The cost of research and development in year 0 would amount to $90 million, and the production costs in year 2 would be $110 million.

    a. Calculate the project's average annual cash flow.
    b. Should Merck accept this project if the cost of capital is 16%?

Answers

True of False Questions

1	F	6	F
2	T	7	T
3	T	8	F
4	F	9	F
5	T	10	F

Multiple Choice Questions

1	C	6	C
2	B	7	A
3	B	8	D
4	A	9	B
5	D	10	D

Questions and Problems

1. Zayre's annual cash flows are:

Year	1	2	3	4
Cash inflows	$600,00	$1,000,00	$1,000,00	$400,000
Cash outflows	-$300,00	-$600,00	-$600,00	-$300,000
Total cash flows	$300,00	$400,00	$400,00	$100,000

The $600,000 cash inflow in year 1 represents 60% of the $1,000,000 sales in year 1. Zayre pays only 50% of the $600,000 cost of goods in cash, so there is a $300,000 cash outflow in year 1. In years 2 and 3, Zayre's cash inflow consists of $600,000 cash payment for the current year's sales plus the $400,000 deferred payment form the previous year's sales. Similarly, the cash outflow consists of $300,000 payment deferred from the previous year. In year 4, the total cash flow is $400,000, cash inflow from year 3 sales minus the $300,000 cost of goods purchased in year 3.

2. a. The annual inflation rate can be computed from the increase in the cost of the TV set:

$3,400 = $3,000 (1+Inflation rate)^2

Inflation rate $= (3,400 / 3,000)^{1/2} - 1 = 6.46\%$

b. The real annual interest rate is given by:

Real rate $= [(1+Nominal rate) / (1+Inflation rate)] - 1$
$\qquad = (1.09 / 1.0646) - 1 = 2.39\%$

3. The firm's annual earnings before tax are $650,000 - $300,000 = $350,000. The $300,000 cost is the annual straight-line depreciation. The tax rate is 35%, so the firm's annual after-tax cash flow will be:

    $(1 - 0.35)\,(\$350,000) = \$227,500$

4. Depreciation expense is tax deductible. The tax paid for Boeing will be ($350,000)(0.35) = $122,500. The firm's annual after tax cash flow will be:
    $650,000 - $122,500 = $527,500

5. The project's NPV at 12% cost of capital is:
    $\text{NPV} = -\$900,000 + \$527,500 / (1.12) + \$527,500 / (1.12)^2 + \$527,500 / (1.12)^3$
    $= -\$900,000 + \$470,982 + \$420,520 + \$375,464 = \$366,968$
    The NPV is positive. Thus the project should be accepted.

6. When accelerated depreciation is allowed, Boeing's earnings change. The after-tax earnings are:

    Year 1: [$650,000 – (0.5 x $900,000] (1-0.35) = $130,000
    Year 2: [$650,000 – (0.3 x $900,000] (1-0.35) = $247,000
    Year 3: [$650,000 – (0.2 x $900,000] (1-0.35) = $305,000

7. The firm's after-tax cash flows are:

    Year 1: [$650,000 – (0.35) ($200,000) = $580,000
    Year 2: [$650,000 – (0.35) ($380,000) = $517,000
    Year 3: [$650,000 – (0.35) ($470,000) = $485,000

8. Yes the accelerated depreciation affect the project's NPV:

    $\text{NPV} = -\$900,000 + \$580,000 / (1.12) + \$517,500 / (1.12)^2 + \$485,000 / (1.12)^3$
    $= -\$900,000 + \$517,857 + \$412,149 + \$345,576 = \$375.582$
    The project should be accepted.

9. a. The side effect of this project must be taken into account in calculating cash flows:

Year	1	2	3	4	5
Cash flow	-600	100	150	200	200
Side effect	0	0	10	15	15
Total	-600	100	160	215	215

At a 9% cost of capital, the NPV of the project is:
$\text{NPV} = -600 + 100 / (1.09) + \$150 / (1.09)^2 + 160 / (1.09)^3 + 215 / (1.09)^4 + 215 / (1.09)^5$

$$= -600 + 91.74 + 126.26 + 123.55 + 152.31 + 139.73$$
$$= \$33.59$$

The project's NPV is positive. Honda should accept the project.

b. If Honda has to spend $20 million on machinery in year 2 to produce the spare parts, the total cash flow in year 2 is $150 - $20 = $130

The NPV of this project is:
$$NPV = -600 + 100 / (1.09) + 130 / (1.09)^2 + 160 / (1.09)^3 + 215 / (1.09)^4 + 215 / (1.09)^5$$
$$= \$16.75$$
The project's NPV is positive. Even if Honda has to spend $20 million in year 2, the firm should accept the project.

10. There are two possible states of nature: In the first state, there is a probability of 30% of the research and development failing. In that case, the firm's cash flow will be (in millions of dollars):

Year	1	2	3	4	5
Cash Flows	-90	0	0	0	0

The R&D investment has been made and there are no further expenses. Because the project is terminated, there are no cash inflows. In the second state, there is probability of 70% of the research and development succeeding. In that case, the firm's cash flows will be:

Year	1	2	3	4	5
Cash Flows	-90	-110	200	200	100

Multiplying each cash flow by its respective probability, and summing, we obtain the following average annual cash flows:

Year	1	2	3	4	5
Cash Flows	-90	-77	140	140	70

For example, the cash flow in year 2 is (30%)(0) + (70%)(200 million) = $140 million.

b. The NPV of the project is:
$$NPV = -90 - 77 / (1.16) + 140 / (1.16)^2 + 70 / (1.16)^3 + 70 / (1.16)^4$$
$$= -90 - 66.38 + 104.05 + 89.70 + 38.66$$
$$= \$76.03$$
The project's NPV is positive. Merck should accept this project.

RISK AND CAPITAL BUDGETING

Chapter Summary

- An all-equity firm can discount its investment projects at the cost of equity, while a firm with both debt and equity in the capital structure should discount its investment using the weighted average cost of capital (WACC).

- The cost of equity of a firm is affected by the firm's operating leverage and financial leverage.

- The WACC is the weighted average of its component cost with the weights equal to the proportion of the market value of each component.

- When a firm wants to make an investment outside of its normal line of business, it should estimate the asset beta for this industry using pure play firms.

- To analyze sources of uncertainty of a project's cash flows, managers can use different tools such as break-even analysis, sensitivity analysis, scenario analysis, Monte Carlo simulations, and decision trees.

- The value of many investments includes not only the NPV, but also the investment's real options. These real options include the option to expand, the option to abandon, the option to make follow–on investments and flexibility options.

True or False Questions

T   F   1. The appropriate discount rate to use in NPV calculations can vary from one investment to another as long as risks vary across investments.

T   F   2. In practice, managers rarely use the CAPM to compute their firm's cost of equity.

T   F   3. When a small percentage decrease in sales leads to a large percentage decrease in EBIT, the firm has low operating leverage.

T   F   4. A firm that has debt in its capital structure cannot discount project cash flows using its equity capital.

T   F   5. The beta on a firm's bonds is low relative to the beta of its common stock.

T   F   6. When a firm uses no leverage, its equity beta equals to its asset beta.

T   F   7. In sensitivity analysis, managers calculate a project NPV when a whole set of assumptions changes in a particular way.

T   F   8. NPV calculations do not take into account actions by managers to increase the value of an investment once it has been made.

T   F   9. An investment's option value, unlike to its NPV, increases as risk increases.

T   F 10. In a market with zero economic profits, the NPV of any investment equals zero because every project earns just enough to recover the cost of capital.

Multiple Choice Questions

1.   A firm with both debt and equity in the capital structure should discount its investment using the:

   a. cost of equity.
   b. cost of debt.
   c. weighted average cost of capital.
   d. marginal cost of capital.

2.   A firm's cost of equity can be estimated using the:

   a. CAPM.
   b. WACC.
   c. marginal cost of capital.
   d. average equity premium.

3.   During the 20th century, the average real return on stock outpaced the average real return on U.S treasury bills by:

   a. 3.4 % per year.
   b. 7.7 % per year.
   c. 5.8 % per year.
   d. 9.1 % per year.

4.   Which of the following is not a tool used by corporate managers to deal with uncertainty of a project's cash flows?

   a. decision trees
   b. Monte Carlo simulations
   c. scenario analyses
   d. real options

5.   Which of the following is not a real option?

        a. flexibility options
        b. option to abandon
        c. executive stock options
        d. option to make follow-on investments

6.   According to a recent survey about the cost of capital in India:

        a. Most Indian firms use the yields on 1-yeargovernment notes to proxy for the
           risk-free rate.
        b. Firms in India use the CAPM more frequently than any other method to
        estimate their cost of equity.
        c. Estimates of the cost of equity capital in India average about 12 percent.
        d. The WACC for Indian companies falls in the 8-12 % range.

7.   A firm's cost of equity is influenced by:

        a. operating leverage only.
        b. financial leverage only.
        c. both operating leverage and financial leverage.
        d. operating leverage, financial leverage, and real options.

8.   In principle, the appropriate discount rate to use in NPV calculations:

        a. is the WACC.
        b. is the cost of equity.
        c. can vary from one investment to another as long as risks vary across
        investments.
        d. is either the cost of equity or the cost of debt.

9.   The tendency of the volatility of operating cash flows to increase with fixed costs
        is measured by:

        a. operating leverage.
        b. total leverage.
        c. financial leverage.
        d. both operating leverage and financial leverage.

10.   When a firm uses no leverage,

        a. its equity beta is greater than its asset beta.
        b. its equity beta equals its asset beta.
        c. the firm is called a pure play.
        d. its equity beta is smaller than its asset beta.

Questions and Problems

1. Coca Cola has a capital structure consisting almost entirely of equity.

   a. If the beta of Coca Cola stock equals 0.9, the risk-free rate equals 4%, and the expected return on the S&P 500 equals 10%, what is the cost of equity of Coca Cola?
   b. Suppose the Federal Reserve cuts the discount rate causing a 1% decrease in the risk-free rate. Holding all other factors constant, how would Coca Cola's cost of equity change?

2. The risk-free rate equals 3 %, and the expected risk premium on the market portfolio equals 7 %. Lockheed has bonds outstanding that offer investors a yield to maturity of 5.8 %. What is the debt beta?

3. Intel's assets have a beta of 1.2. Assume that the debt beta equals 0.0 and that there are no corporate income taxes, calculate Intel's equity beta under the following assumptions:

   a. Intel's capital structure is 100% equity.
   b. The capital structure is 30% debt and 70% equity.
   c. The capital structure is 50% debt and 50% equity.
   d. The capital structure is 70% debt and 30% equity.

   Do you believe that the assumption of a zero debt beta is equally valid for each of these capital structures? Why of why not?

4. Two stocks, Kraft and Sysco, have a beta equal to 0.9. However, Sysco's standard deviation is 5% larger than the standard deviation of Kraft. Which stock is more risky?

5. Hewlett Packard, an all equity firm, has a market value of $3 billion. Its beta is 1. The market portfolio's average rate of return is 14% and the risk-free rate of interest is 6%/ Hewlett Packard is considering buying Compaq, which has a beta of 1.3. The required outlay to buy Compaq is $1 billion.

   a. Calculate the cost of capital of Hewlett Packard
   b. What is the cost of capital of Compaq?
   c. What is the new beta of Hewlett Packard after buying Compaq?
   d. Should Hewlett Packard buy Compaq if the IRR of the project is 16%?

6. Cummins Engine Corporation has fixed costs of $300 million per year. Across all the firm's products, the average contribution margin equals $900. What is Cumming Engine's break-even point in terms of units sold?

7.   Suppose that the aggregate dividend yield on stocks is 2% and is constant over time. The long-term (real) growth rate of aggregate dividends is 3.6%. What is the expected real return on stocks?

The following data apply to the next three questions.

The value of AMD is $900 million. The value of debt is $180 million on which 9% interest is payable. The pre-tax average cash flow is $160 million and the marginal tax rate is 35%.

8.   What is the cost of equity of AMD?

9.   What is the after-tax cost of debt of AMD?

10.   Compute the WACC of AMD.

Solutions

True of False Questions

1	T	6	T
2	F	7	F
3	F	8	T
4	T	9	T
5	T	10	T

Multiple Choice Questions

1	c	6	b
2	a	7	c
3	b	8	c
4	d	9	a
5	c	10	b

Questions and Problems

1. a. The cost of equity of Coca Cola is:
    4% + (10% - 4%) (0.9) = 9.4%.

    b. The new cost of equity of Coca Cola is:
    3% + (10% - 3%) (0.9) = 9.3%.

2. The debt beta is:
    $5.8\% = 3\% + \beta_d \, 7\%$
    $\beta_d = 0.4$.

3. Intel' s equity beta is:
    a.   1.2.

    b. $1.2 = (0) (0.3) + \beta_E (0.7)$
    $\beta_E = 1.71$.

    c. $1.2 = (0) (0.5) + \beta_E (0.5)$
    $\beta_E = 2.4$.

    d. $1.2 = (0) (0.7) + \beta_E (0.3)$
    $\beta_E = 4.0$.

The assumption that the debt beta is zero no matter how much the firm borrows is unreasonable. The more the firm borrows, the riskier its debt is and the debt beta must be higher.

4. If your portfolio consists of only one stock, then standard deviation is the proper measure of risk, and Sysco is the more risky stock. However, if you are adding another stock to your well-diversified portfolio, beta is the proper measure of risk, and Kraft and Sysco are equally risky.

5. a. The cost of capital of Hewlett Packard is:
    6% + (14% - 6%) (1.0) = 14.0%.

    b. The cost of capital of Compaq is:
    6% + (14% - 6%) (1.3) = 16.4%.

    c. The new beta of Hewlett Packard after buying Compaq is:
    β = ($3 billion / $4billion) x 1.0 + ($1 billion / $4billion) x 1.3
       = 0.75 +0.325 = 1.075.

    d. The cost of capital of Hewlett Packard after buying Compaq is:
    6% + (14% - 6%) (1.075) = 14.6%.

    e. Hewlett Packard should not buy Compaq because the IRR of the project is smaller that the cost of capital of 16.4%.

6. The break even point for Cummings Engine is:
    $300 million / $900 = 333,333 units.

7. The expected real return on stocks is the sum of the dividend yield and the real growth rate in dividends. In this case, that sum is 2% + 3.6% = 5.6%.

8. The cost of equity of AMD is:
    $$Re = \frac{(1-T)\ (X-rD)}{E} = \frac{(1-0.35)\ [\$160 - (9\%)(180)]}{\$720}$$

    = (0.65) ($143.8) / $720 = 12.98%.

9. The after tax cost of debt of AMD is:
    9% (1-0.35) = 5.85%.

10. The WACC of AMD is:
    (12.98%) (0.8) + (5.85%) (0.2) = 11.55%.

10

MARKET EFFICIENCY AND MODERN FINANCIAL MANAGEMENT

Chapter Summary

- Financial markets tend to be more competitive and efficient than product markets.

- An allocatively efficient market ensures that capital is invested productively. An operationally efficient market is one where outputs are produced at the lowest possible costs. An informationally efficient market is the market in which asset prices adjust quickly and fully to relevant new information.

- In weak-form efficient markets, security prices reflect all information available in the record of historical prices, while semi-strong-form efficient markets reflect all publicly available information. In strong-firm efficient markets, prices reflect all information, including inside information.

- Empirical research has generally found that the major Western stock and bond markets are weak-form and semi-strong-form efficient, but not strong-form efficient.

- Although some empirical studies find that certain types of financial asset returns are partly predictable, the extent of predictability is modest.

- Research in behavioral finance claims that investors make systematic errors in valuing assets due to cognitive problems such as overconfidence and self-attribution bias. If the biases are widespread, they can cause security prices to deviate from fundamental value for long periods of time.

True or False Questions

T   F   1. Financial markets offer creative financial managers as many positive NPV investment opportunities as product markets do.

T   F   2. Allocative efficiency determines whether markets produce outputs at the lowest possible cost.

T   F   3. The strong-form efficiency asserts that security prices incorporate all publicly available information.

T   F   4. Trading rules based on return continuations are called momentum strategies or underreaction strategies.

T   F   5. The empirical evidence suggests that the advice offered by security analysts does not allow investors to consistently beat the market portfolio of stocks.

T   F   6. In general, behavioral finance offers no specific theory to counter the efficient market hypothesis.

T   F   7. Both overconfidence and self-attribution bias cause investors to overreact to new information.

T   F   8. Behavioral finance claims that financial markets are irrationally volatile and are prone to recurring bubbles, facts, and information cascades.

T   F   9. Empirical evidence documents that hedge funds consistently outperform mutual funds and standard market indexes.

T   F   10. Empirical studies indicate that insiders do earn excess returns on their trades, contrary to strong-form market efficiency.

Multiple Choice Questions

1.   Which form of market efficiency asserts that asset prices incorporate all publicly available information?

    a. allocative efficiency
    b. strong-form efficiency
    c. semistrong-form efficiency
    d. weak-form efficiency

2.   Over the three-year period leading up to March 2000, the Nasdaq Composite Index increased by:

    a. 250%
    b. 300%
    c. 400%
    d. 600%

3.   What kind of efficiency determines whether markets produce outputs at the lowest possible cost?

    a. Operational efficiency
    b. Allocative efficiency
    c. Informational efficiency
    d. Strong-form efficiency

4.   Trading rules based on return continuations are called:

a. underreaction strategies.
b. overrreaction strategies.
c. filter rules.
d. fundamental analysis.

5.   Overconfidence causes investors to:

a. underreact to new information.
b. overreact to new information.
c. adjust quickly to new information.
d. respond gradually to new information.

6.   Empirical tests of mutual fund investment performance are tests of:

a. weak-form market efficiency.
b. semistrong-form market efficiency.
c. strong-form market efficiency.
d. allocative efficiency.

7.   According to a recent survey about the cost of capital in India:

a. Most Indian firms use the yields on 1-year..
b. Firms in India use the CAPM more frequently than any other method to estimate their cost of equity.
c. Estimates of the cost of equity capital in India average about 12 percent.
d. The WACC for Indian companies falls in the 8-12 % range.

8.   Most empirical studies find that asset prices:

a. underreact to new information.
b. overreact to new information.
c. respond fully and nearly instantaneously to new information .
d. respond gradually to new information.

9.   Which of the following tests is a test of semistrong-form market efficiency?

a. test of pension fund and hedge fund investment performance
b. test of serial correlation in stock returns
c. test for the effectiveness and technical analysis
d. test for rational information processing

10.   Which of the following investment funds are largely unregulated:

a. pension funds
b. mutual funds
c. closed-end funds
d. hedge funds

Questions and Problems

1.   Suppose you find that a 10% filter rule consistently generates significant profits after transaction costs. Is it a violation of the EMH?

2.   Which of the following phenomena would be either consistent with or a violation of the EMH? Explain.

a. Hedge funds consistently outperform mutual funds, but not standard market indexes.
b. Insiders consistently learn excess returns on their trades after transaction costs.
c. Stocks that perform well in one month perform poorly in the following month.

3.   A successful firm like General Electric has generated large profits for years. Is this a violation of the EMH?

4.   The regression of General Motors stock against the return for the Standard and Poor's 500 Index gives the following result"
$$r_{GM} = 0.21 + 1.05 \, r_{S\&P}$$
If the market return is 13% and the GM return is 16%, what is the excess return for GM? $16 - [0.21 + 1.05(0.13)] \Rightarrow 18.65\%$
$16 - [0.3465$
13% not 0.13

The following data apply to the next four problems.

Assume the following prices of Microsoft are:

Day	Stock Price
0	$25
1	26
2	28
3	31
4	30
5	28
6	30
7	31
8	30
9	28
10	27

5.   If you follow the strategy if using a 1% filter rule, on what days would you buy Microsoft stock?

6.   On what day would you sell and short Microsoft stock?

7.   Ignoring transaction costs, what is the rate of return you can earn by following the 1% filter rule?

8.   What is the rate of return you can earn from buying the stock on day 0 and selling it on day 10?

9.   Suppose Wal-Mart stock has a beta of 1.0. You want to measure the cumulative abnormal return (CAR) of Wal-Mart over a period of time. Find the weekly abnormal return and CAR by filling in the missing values in the following table:

Week	Stock Return (%)	Market Return (%)	Weekly Abnormal Return	CAR
1	1.50	1.41	---	---
2	-0.19	0.08	---	---
3	0.34	-0.12	---	---
4	0.56	0.73	---	---
5	-0.92	-0.65	---	---

10.   Does the random-walk theory suggest that security price levels are random?

Solutions

True or False Questions

1	F	6	T
2	F	7	F
3	F	8	T
4	T	9	F
5	T	10	T

Multiple Choice Questions

1	c	6	c
2	b	7	a
3	a	8	c
4	a	9	d
5	b	10	d

Questions and Problems

1.   If a 10% filter rule consistently generates significant profits after transaction costs, it is a violation of the weak-form market efficiency.

2.   a. It is not a violation of the EMH because hedge funds do not outperform standard market indexes.
b. If insiders consistently earn excess return on their trades after transaction costs, this evidence is a violation of the strong-form market efficiency.
c. This evidence implies that you can predict the future stock performance by observing the previous month stock performance. Therefore, it is a violation of the weak-form market efficiency.

3.   No. General Electric's large profits for many years do not imply that investors who buy GE stock after its success already was evident would earn an abnormal rate of return.

4.   The abnormal return for GM is:
16% - [0.21 + (1.05)(13%)] = 2.14%.

5.   You buy Microsoft stock on days 1 and 6 because the stock increases by at least 1% from the previous of low price. Note that you do not buy additional shares if you already have a long position.

6.   You sell and short the stock on days 4 and 8 because the stock declines by at least 1% from the previous high price.

7.   The rate of return for long positions is:
        15% (day 1 to day 4) + 0% (day 6 to day 8) = 15%.
        The rate of return for short positions is:
        0% (day 4 to day 6) + 10% (day 8 to day 10) = 10%.
        The rate of return you earn by following the 1% filter rule is:
        15% + 10% = 25%.

8.   The rate of return you earn from buying the stock from day 0 and selling it on day
        10 is:
        ($27 - $25) / .25 = 8%.

9.

Week	Stock Return (%)	Market Return (%)	Weekly Abnormal Return	CAR
1	1.50	1.41	0.09	0.09
2	-0.19	0.08	-0.27	-0.18
3	0.34	-0.12	0.46	0.28
4	0.56	0.73	0.17	0.11
5	-0.92	-0.65	-0.27	-0.16

10. No. The random-walk theory suggests that changes in security price are random, not
security price levels are random.

11

AN OVERVIEW OF LONG-TERM FINANCING

Chapter Summary

- The three basic instruments of long-term financing are common stock, preferred stock, and long-term debt.

- In most countries, internally generated funds (retained earnings) are the dominant source of funding for corporations. In these countries, external financing is used only when needed, and debt is preferred to common stock financing.

- Financial intermediaries are institutions that raise funds by selling claims on themselves and use the money to buy debt and equity of claims of corporations.

- Although financial intermediaries are important in the corporate financial systems of most foreign countries, intermediaries play a relatively small direct role in financing for American corporations.

- An effective system of corporate governance significantly affects the financial performance of firms as well as entire economies. Countries with legal systems based on English common law tend to have larger stock and bond markets than countries with other types of legal systems.

True or False Questions

T   F   1. United States has a stock market-based financing system.

T   F   2. Corporate financial systems of industrialized countries with legal systems based on German or French civil law tend to have large stock and bond markets.

T   F   3. Most US Corporations have a majority voting system, which allows each shareholder to cast one vote per share for each open position on the board of directors.

T   F   4. Preferred shareholders typically have voting rights, just like common shareholders.

T   F   5. Most publicly traded bonds issued by American corporations are secured debt.

T   F   6. Financial intermediaries provide a variety of financial service to corporations, but the most important is information intermediation.

T   F 7. Most Western countries and the United States allow commercial banks to act as true merchant banks capable of providing a full range of financial services.

T   F 8. A foreign bond is a single-currency bond sold in several countries simultaneously.

T   F 9. Corporate ownership is likely to be much less concentrated in common law countries than in other advanced economies.

T   F 10. No comparable period in financial history had a dramatic increase in takeover activity as did the 1992 – 2000 period.

Multiple Choice Questions

1. Most US corporations have:

    a. a cumulative voting system.
    b. a majority voting system
    c. two or more outstanding classes of stocks
    d. both preferred stock and common stock

2. Most of the publicly traded bonds issued by American corporations are:

    a. debentures.
    b. secured debt.
    c. equipment trust receipts.
    d. floating-rate bonds.

3. Which of the following statements about preferred stock is false?

    a. Preferred shareholders typically do not have voting rights.
    b. Firms generally do not issue large quantities of preferred stock.
    c. Preferred stockholders hold claims that are senior to those held by bondholders.
    d. A large fraction of the dividends that corporations holding preferred shares receive are tax deductible.

4. Which of the following is not a financial intermediary?

    a. commercial banks
    b. mutual funds
    c. insurance companies
    d. public utilities

5. In the United States, commercial banks are allowed to:

    a. underwrite securities.
    b. provide direct private placement of stock.
    c. make direct equity investments in commercial firms.
    d. lend money to foreign governments.

6. A single-currency bond sold in several countries simultaneously is called a:

    a. Eurobond
    b. foreign bond
    c. Yankee bond
    d. samurai bond

7. Which country has the highest percentage of people age 65+ relative to those of working age?

    a. United States
    b. Sweden
    c. Germany
    d. Japan

8. Which law offers the greatest protection to external creditors and minority shareholders?

    a. French Civil Law
    b. English Common Law
    c. German Law
    d. Scandinavian Law

9. Which of the following statements is false?

    a. Corporate ownership is likely to be much less concentrated in common-law countries than in other advanced economies.
    b. German law offers the weakest legal protections to outside investors.
    c. Ownership structures have become much less concentrated in continental Europe since the mid 1990s.
    d. An effective system of corporate governance significantly impacts the financial performance of individual companies.

10. Which of the following statements is true?

    a. In recent years, US corporate issues account for two-thirds of the worldwide total.
    b. American companies issue more equity than debt each year.
    c. Straight debt represents about 70% of the total capital raised by US companies in recent years.
    d. Initial public offerings account for over half of common stock issued by companies in recent years.

Questions and Problems

1. How many shares are needed to elect three directors out of a slate of ten if a firm has 20 million of shares outstanding and uses cumulative voting in its election?

2. The stockholders' equity section of the balance sheet for CME shows:

Common stock, $0.40 par	$680,00
Additional paid-in capital	$19,920,000
Retained earnings	$28,365,00

   a. How many shares has CME issued?
   b. What is the book value per share?
   c. CME has made only one offering of common stock. At what price did CME sell shares to the market?

3. Last year Big Joe Corporation conducted an IPO, issuing 5 million common shares with a par value of $0.40 to investors at a price of $20 per share. During its first year of operation, Big Joe earned net income of $0.12 per share and paid a dividend of $0.01 per share. At the end of the year, the company's stock was selling for $26 per share. Construct the stockholders' equity account for Big Joe at the end of its first year in business, and calculate the firm's market capitalization.

4. MBI Company is going to elect seven board members. You own 13% of the total shares outstanding. How confident are you to be elected as director under the cumulative voting rule?

5. An election is being held to fill four seats on the board of directors of a small firm in which you hold stock. There are 1,500 shares outstanding. If the election is conducted under cumulative voting and you own 260 shares, how many more shares must you buy to ensure a board seat?

6. The shareholders of Motivational Tapes, Inc. will elect nine board members next month. There are 1,500,000 shares outstanding and the current share price is $9.50. If the election is conducted under cumulative voting, how much will it cost to guarantee yourself one seat on the board?

The following data apply to the next four problems.

The stockholders' equity section of the balance sheet for Brown Company shows:

Common stock, $2 par	566,400
Additional paid-in capital	6,138,600
Retained earnings	9,259,100
Total	16,234,100

7. How many shares did Brown Company issue?

8. At what average price were the shares sold?

9. What is the book value per share?

10. Brown Company decides to issue 50,000 shares of new stock. The current price is $85 per share. Show the effect of the new issue on the equity accounts.

SOLUTIONS

True of False Questions

1	F	6	T
2	F	7	F
3	T	8	F
4	F	9	T
5	F	10	T

Multiple Choice Questions

1	B	6	A
2	A	7	B
3	C	8	B
4	D	9	B
5	D	10	A

Questions and Problems

1. The number of votes required to elect three directors under cumulative voting is:
    NV = [(# of shares outstanding x 3) / (# of director positions +1)] +1
    = [(20,000 x 3) / (10+1)] +1
    = (60,000 / 11) +1
    = 5,454,546 shares required to ensure election of three directors.

2. a. The number of shares issued by CME is:
    $680,000 / $0.4 0 par value per share = 1,700,000.

    b. The total book value of CME common stock is:
    $680,00 + $19,920,000 + $28,365,000 = $48,965,00.
    The book value per share is:
    $48,965,000 / 1,700,000 = $28.80.

    d. The price that CME sold shares to the market is:
    ($680,000 + 19,920,000) / 1,700,000 = $12.12.

3. Immediately after the IPO, the company's equity account is:

Common stock ($0.40 x 5 million)	$2,000,000
Paid-in capital ($20 - $0.40) x 5million	82,000,000
Retained earnings	0
Total stockholders' equity	$84,000,000

After the first year's net income (after dividend payments) are credited to Big Joe's balance sheet, the equity account is:

Common stock	$2,000,000
Paid-in capital	82,000,000
Retained earnings ($0.12 - $0.01) x 5million	550,000
Total stockholders' equity	$84,550,000

Big Joe's market capitalization at the end of the first year is:
$26 x 5 million shares = $130 million.

4. The percentage of the shares you must have to assure a board seat is more than:

$$\frac{1}{\text{(The number of board members being elected} +1)}$$

The lowest percentage of shares you need to win a board seat out of seven is higher than $1/8 = 12.5\%$. Your current ownership of 13% is more than enough to ensure one seat.

5. You currently own 260 shares or 17.33% of the outstanding shares. You need to control 1/5 of the votes, which requires 300 shares. You need 41 additional shares to elect yourself to the board.

6. You need just over $1/(9+1)$ or 10% of the outstanding shares. At $9.5 per share it will cost you $9.5 x 150,000 shares = $1,425,000 to guarantee yourself a board seat.

7. The number of shares that Brown Company issued is:
$566,400 / $2 = 283,200 shares.

8. The average price that the shares are sold is:
($566,400 + $6,138,600) / 283,200 = $23.68.

9. The total book value of Brown Company common stock is:
$566,400 + 6,138,600 + 9,529,100 = $16,234,100.
The book value per share is:
$16,234,100 / 283,200 = 57.32.

10. Common stock (333,200 shares outstanding, $2 par)

Common stock (333,200 shares outstanding, $2 par)	$664,400
Additional paid-in capital ($20 - $0.40) x 5million	10,288,600
Retained earnings	9,529,100
Total	$20,482,100

Note: The new additional paid-in capital is:
$6,138,600 + [($85 -$2) x 50,000] = $10,288,600.

12

CAPITAL STRUCTURE: THEORY AND TAXES

Chapter Summary

- The capital structure ratio measures the ratio of a firm's long-term debt to its equity capital.

- In general, industries rich in fixed assets tend to have higher leverage, while industries rich in intangible assets tend to have lower leverage.

- In countries where bankruptcy laws favor creditors, especially Britain and Germany, market-value leverage ratios tend to be lower than in countries where debtors enjoy greater bankruptcy protection.

- Modigliani and Miller (M&M) develop a model showing that capital structure is irrelevant in a world of frictionless capital markets.

- In the M&M model with corporate taxes, the optimal strategy is to use the maximum possible leverage.

- When corporate profits are taxed at both the corporate and personal levels, the benefits of high levels of corporate debts are reduced and may be negative. (Note that recent proposed tax legislation would eliminate or greatly reduce corporate taxes.)

True or False Questions

T   F   1. Highly-levered industries include utilities, transportation, and mining.

T   F   2. Within industries, leverage varies inversely with profitability.

T   F   3. The stock market generally responds favorably when firms take actions that increase leverage.

T   F   4. The trade-off model can be used to explain why firms hold vast amounts of cash and marketable securities.

T   F   5. The signaling theory assumes that managers know more about a firm's prospects than investors do.

T   F   6. The M&M model with corporate taxes claims that the market value of any firm is independent of its capital structure.

T   F   7. Municipal bonds are issued by U.S state and federal governments.

T   F   8. The nondebt tax shields hypothesis states that companies with large amounts of depreciation, investment tax credits and R&D expenditures should use more debt financing than similar firms with fewer such shields.

T   F   9. The higher the personal tax rate on interest income, the lower will be the equilibrium leverage level.

T   F   10. In general, industries rich in intangible assets tend to have lower leverage.

Multiple Choice Questions

1. Which of the following countries has the highest long-term debt to total capital ratio:

    a. United Kingdom
    b. Italy
    c. United States
    d. South Korea

2. Which of the following firms tends to use more debt in the capital structure?

    a. firms with high-value intangible assets
    b. firms with high profitability
    c. firms with high market-to-book ratios
    d. firms with larger perceived costs of financial distress

3. Empirical evidence indicates that stock prices decline when a company announces:

    a. debt-for-equity exchange offers.
    b. acquisition offers involving payment with the company's own assets.
    c. debt-financed share repurchase programs.
    d. debt-financed cash tender offers to acquire control of another company.

4. Which of the following capital structure theories can explain why firms hold vast amount of cash and marketable securities?

    a. the trade-off model
    b. the pecking order hypothesis
    c. the signaling model of corporate financial structure
    d. the M&M capital structure model

5. The conclusion that the optimal leverage ratio for any firm is 100% debt is consistent with:

    a. the M&M model with corporate taxes.
    b. the M&M model with corporate and personal taxes.
    c. the trade-off model.
    d. the pecking order hypothesis.

6. Which of the following countries has the highest personal income tax rate:

    a. Japan
    b. Germany
    c. France
    d. Netherlands

7. When is the equilibrium leverage level economy-wide lower?

    a. The personal tax rate on interest income is higher.
    b. The corporate income tax rate is higher.
    c. The personal tax rate on equity-related investment income is higher.
    d. The personal tax rate on dividend is higher.

8. Which of the following statements is not a conclusion reached by the M&M capital structure model with no corporate income taxes?

    a. Capital structure does not matter.
    b. The values of two similar firms, one levered and one unlevered, will be equal.
    c. The cost of equity increases with leverage.
    d. Leverage has no effect on the cost of equity.

9. The optimal capital structure:

    a. minimizes the cost of capital.
    b. does not matter in the real world.
    c. is not affected by characteristics of a firm's assets.
    d. can be found by using a mathematical formula.

10. The M&M model with corporate taxes claims that:

    a. the capital structure does not matter.
    b. firms should pay attention to bankruptcy cost.
    c. the higher the proportion of debt in the firm's capital structure, the larger the firm's value.
    d. a firm should seek an optimal financial mix, which will not ordinarily consist entirely of debt.

Questions and Problems

1. A firm operates in perfect capital markets. The cost of debt is 5%, the cost of equity is 12%, and the WACC is 9%. What is the firm's debt-to-equity ratio?

2. Describe three main conclusions of the M&M capital structure model in a perfect capital market.

3. Two firms are identical in all respects except that one is levered and the other is not. Suppose that there are no taxes and the all-equity firm's cost of capital is 12%. The interest rate is 9%. Now assume that the interest rate falls to 7% and business risk increases so that the unlevered firm's cost of equity remains 12%.

   a. What is the rate of return on the levered firm's equity before and after the drop in the interest rate? Assume the debt-to-equity ratio is 1.
   b. Does the levered firm's value change with the reduction in interest rate? Explain.
   c. Does the levered firm's WACC change? Explain.

   The following data apply to the next three problems:

   Two firms are identical in all respects except that one is levered and the other is not. Suppose that there are no taxes and the all-equity firm's cost of capital is 10%. The levered firm has $20 million of 8% bonds outstanding. The EBIT is $4 million.

4. What is the value of the levered firm?

5. What is the cost of equity of the levered firm?

6. What is the WACC of the levered firms?

7. A firm's net operating income will be -$40 million or $20 million with equal probability. The levered firm's value is $1 million. An otherwise identical firm issues $400 million debt at 6%.

   a. Calculate the rate of return of the levered firm.
   b. Calculate the mean and standard deviation of the unlevered firm's rate of return on equity.
   c. Calculate the mean and standard deviation of the levered firm's rate of return on equity.

The following data apply to the next three problems:

An unlevered firm's NOI would be $1 million, $3 million, or $5 million, with equal probabilities. The firm issues two million shares, and its cost of capital is 10%.

8. What is the value of this unlevered firm?

9. What would the firm's value be if it were levered? Assume the corporate tax rate is 40%, the interest rate is 6%, and the debt is $10 million.

10. What would be the levered firm's stock price be if it had issued three million shares? Does the number of shares issued affect the levered firm's value?

SOLUTIONS

True of False Questions

1	F	6	F
2	T	7	F
3	T	8	F
4	F	9	T
5	T	10	T

Multiple Choice Questions

1	D	6	D
2	C	7	A
3	B	8	D
4	B	9	A
5	A	10	C

Questions and Problems

1. The expected return on a levered firm's equity is:
    $r_l = r + (r-r_d) \times D/E$
    $0.12 = 0.09 + (0.09 - 0.05) \times D/E$
    $0.12 - 0.09 = (0.09 - 0.05) \times D/E$
    $0.03 = 0.04\ D/E$
    The debt to equity ratio is:
    $D/E = 0.03 / 0.04 = 0.75$.

2. Modigliani and Miller reach three main conclusions:
    - Leverage has no effect on the firms' value.
    - The cost of equity increases with leverage.
    - Leverage has no effect on the WACC.

3. a. $r_l = r + (r-r_d) \times D/E$
    Before the interest change, $r_l = 12\% + (12\% - 9\%)(1) = 15\%$.
    After the interest change, $r_l = 12\% + (12\% - 7\%)(1) = 17\%$.
    b. No, we know that the value of the unlevered firm is constant (its NOI and cost of capital are constant). Therefore, the value of the levered firm must also be constant or arbitrage will occur.
    c. No, the WACC of the levered firm is equal to the cost of capital of the unlevered firm, which remains constant.

4. The value of the levered firm is:
    $V_L = V_U = \$4$ million $/ 0.1 = \$40$ million.

5. The cost of equity of the levered firm is:
$r_l = r + (r-r_d) \times D/E$
$= 10\% + (10\% - 8\%) (20/20) = 12\%$.

6. The WACC of the levered firm is:
$WACC = (8\%)(0.5) + (12\%)(0.5) = 10\%$.

7. a. The rate of the unlevered firm is either -4%, (-$40 million / $ 1 billion) or 20% ($200 million / $1 billion) with equal probability.
The rate of return of the levered firm is:

	State 1	State 2
NOI	-$40	$200
Interest ($400 at 6%)	-24	-24
Net Income	-64	176
Rate of Return (net income /equity)	-10.67%	29.33%

b. The mean rate of return of the unlevered firm is:
$(-4\%)(0.5) + (20\%)(0.5) = 0.8\%$.
The variance of return of the unlevered firm is:
$\sigma^2 = (-4-12)^2 (0.5) + (20-12)^2(0.5) = 160$.
The standard deviation is:
$\sigma = (160)^{1/2} = 12.65\%$.
c. The mean rate of return of the unlevered firm is:
$(-10.67\%)(0.5) + (29.33\%)(0.5) = 9.33\%$.
The variance of return of the levered firm is:
$\sigma^2 = (-10.67-9.33)^2 (0.5) + (29.33-9.33)^2(0.5) = 400$.
The standard deviation is:
$\sigma = (400)^{1/2} = 20\%$.

8. The expected NOI is:
($1 million + $3 million + $5 million) (1/3) = $3 million.
The value of the unlevered firm is:
$V_u = \dfrac{NOI\ (1-T_c)}{r} = \dfrac{(\$3\ million)\ (1-0.4)}{0.1} = \$18\ million$.

9. The value of the levered firm is:
$V_L = V_u + T_cD = \$18\ million + (0.4)\ (\$10\ million) = \$22\ million$.

10. The levered firm's equity is:
$EL = VL - D = \$22\ million - \$10\ million = \$12\ million$.
The levered firm's stock price is:
$12 million / 3 million = $4.
No, the number of shares has no impact on the aggregate value of the equity or the value of the levered firm.

13

CAPITAL STRUCTURE: NONTAX DETERMINANTS OF CORPORATE LEVERAGE

Chapter Summary

- The level of debt that a firm uses is influenced by not only the corporate and personal taxation of income, but also by characteristics of the firm's asset structure, ownership structure, operating environment, and investment opportunities.

- Firms with large amounts of tangible assets tend to use a large amount of debt in the capital structure. In contrast, firms that have more intangible assets tend to use very little financial leverage.

- There are agency costs inherent in the relationship between corporate managers and outside investors. In some cases, using financial leverage can reduce these agency problems; in others, use of leverage exacerbates the problems.

- The pecking order theory predicts that managers will operate their firms in such a way as to minimize the need for outside financing. These managers will use the safest source of funding when they must secure external financing.

- The signaling theory predicts that managers will select the leverage level to signal to outside investors that the firm is strong enough to use high debt and still fund its profitable investment projects.

- The trade-off model of capital structure posits that managers choose the mix of debt and equity that strikes a balance between the tax advantages of debt and the various costs of using leverage.

- Most of the empirical research tends to support the trade-off theory over the pecking order or signaling theory.

True or False Questions

T   F   1. A bankrupt company's security holders, even senior bondholders, can lose their entire investment in a firm.

T   F   2. Bankruptcy is the result of economic failure, not the cause.

T   F   3. Companies whose assets are mostly intangible tend to use a large amount of debt in the capital structure.

T F 4. Both levered and unlevered firms are vulnerable to the asset substitution problem and to the underinvestment problem.

T F 5. Indirect bankruptcy costs are expenses that result from bankruptcy, including cash expenses spent on the process itself.

T F 6. Even though signaling models have intuitive appeal, they enjoy less empirical support than either the trade-off or pecking order theories.

T F 7. Selling stock to outside investors creates agency costs of equity, which are borne by the entrepreneur, but do not harm society as a whole.

T F 8. Highly profitable firms tend to use less debt than do less profitable ones.

T F 9. Empirical studies document a positive relation between leverage and the market-to-book ratio.

T F 10. Entrenched managers tend to employ little debt, even when this policy is harmful to shareholders.

Multiple Choice Questions

1. Which of the following is not an example of market imperfections that could influence capital structures?

    a. A firm's investment opportunities must be unrelated to the firm's use of leverage.
    b. There must be significant costs to bankruptcy or financial distress.
    c. There must be significant costs to negotiating contracts between managers, stockholders, and creditors.
    d. It is costly to credibly convey information about a firm's future prospects between interested parties.

2. Which of the following countries has the highest ratio of R&D spending to GDP?

    a. United States
    b. Japan
    c. Germany
    d. Sweden

3. Which of the following is not a direct cost of bankruptcy?

    a. document printing and filing expenses
    b. lost sales during and after the bankruptcy
    c. lawyer fees
    d. professional fees paid to investment bankers

4. The percent of company's shares owned by managers and directors of most Fortune 500 companies is about:

    a. 5 percent.
    b. 10 percent.
    c. 13 percent.
    d. 17 percent.

5. The typical compensation of CEO's in Fortune 500 companies in salary, bonuses, and stock options is about:

    a. $1 million per year.
    b. $3 million per year.
    c. $6 million per year.
    d. $9 million per year.

6. Which of the following firms tend to use less debt in capital structure?

    a. firms in regulated industries.
    b. firms that have high market-to-book ratio.
    c. state-owned enterprises.
    d. large, more established firms.

7. Which of the following variables has an insignificant relation with financial leverage?

    a. insider share ownership
    b. personal tax rate on equity income
    c. managerial entrenchment
    d. earnings volatility

8. Financial leverage has positive relation with:

    a. nondebt tax shields.
    b. creditor power in bankruptcy.
    c. asset tangibility.
    d. profitability.

9. Which of the following theories assumes that a firm's managers know more about the company's future prospects than do outside investors?

    a. the pecking order hypothesis
    b. the trade-off theory of corporate leverage
    c. the M&M theory with corporate and personal taxes
    d. the M&M theory with corporate taxes

10. Which of the following statements is false?

    a. The pecking order theory cannot explain all the capital structure regularities observed in practice.
    b. A signal is an action that has low cost to the sender, but credibly conveys information to uninformed outsiders.
    c. Agency costs for managers and stockholders are real and are very difficult to reduce effectively.
    d. Highly profitable firms tend to use less debt than do less profitable ones.

Questions and Problems

1. Ryder's balance sheet shows debt of $90 million. This amount is also the debt's market value. The firm has 20 million outstanding shares, and the market price per share is $32. In 2003, Ryder considers issuing $70 million more debt to raise its total debt to $160 million. The firm plans to use the additional cash to repurchase stock. Management estimates that the stock will jump to $35 per share as a result of the change in the capital structure. Therefore, Ryder repurchases 2 million shares.

    a. What is Ryder's debt/equity ratio before the change in the capital structure?
    b. What is Ryder's market value before the change in the capital structure?
    c. What is the market value of Ryder after the leverage is increased?
    d. Suppose the CEO of Ryder decides not to increase debt. What agency cost will Ryder incur?

2. Are the direct costs of financial distress likely to be higher for:

    a. a company that has three publicly traded bonds outstanding or a similar company that borrows from two local banks.
    b. a grocery store that has accounts payable to 200 vendors or a similar sized bookstore that has four accounts payable to suppliers.
Explain.

3. Are the indirect costs of financial distress likely to be higher for:

    a. an Internet company or railroad company.
    b. a pharmaceutical company or an automobile manufacturing company.

    Explain.

4. American Airlines experiences financial distress with $950 million in debt outstanding that will mature in four months. The firm has $500 million cash on hand. You are the CEO of American Airlines and you want to maximize the wealth of shareholders. The bond covenants prevent you from paying out the cash to shareholders as cash dividends. What action should you take to maximize the wealth of shareholders?

The following information applies to the next problems.

Anixter is an unleveraged firm. It has constant EBIT of $20 million per year. The firm's tax rate is 40%, and its market value is $120 million. Anixter is planning to issue a bond and use the proceeds to buy back stock so that the size of the company will remain the same. Because interest expense is tax deductible, the value of Anixter would increase when debt is used, but there could be an offset in the form of rising risk of financial distress. Anixter estimates that the present value of financial distress costs is $80 million and the probability of distress would increase with leverage according to the following table:

Value of Debt	Probability of Financial Distress
$25 million	0.00%
50 million	1.25
75 million	2.50
100 million	6.25
125 million	12.50
150 million	31.25
200 million	75.00

5. What is Anixter's cost of equity before the use of debt financing?

6. What is the optimal level of debt under M&M model with corporate taxes but without financial distress costs? What is the maximum value of Anixter?

7. Prepare a table showing the value of Anixter with various level of debt when financial distress costs are present.

8. With financial distress costs, what is the optimal debt level? What is the optimal debt-to-total asset ratio?

9. What is the maximum value of the firm when financial distress costs are included?

10. Compare the maximum value of the firm with and without distress costs.

SOLUTIONS

True of False Questions

1	T	6	T
2	T	7	F
3	F	8	T
4	F	9	F
5	F	10	T

Multiple Choice Questions

1	A	6	B
2	D	7	A
3	B	8	C
4	A	9	A
5	D	10	B

Questions and Problems

1. a. Ryder's debt/equity ratio before the change in capital structure is:
   $90 million / (20 million) ($32) = 14.1%.
   b. The market value of Ryder before the change in capital structure is:
   $90 million + (20 million) ($32) = $730 million.
   c. The market value of Ryder after the leverage is increased is:
   $160 million + (18 million) ($35) = $790 million.
   d. The agency costs are:
   $790 million - $730 million = $60 million.

2. a. A company with publicly traded bonds is likely to have higher direct costs of financial distress because bondholders may not be able to enforce their claims as effectively as the local bankers who are private lenders.
   b. The grocery store is likely to have higher direct costs of financial distress because it is more difficult to sort out the claims of a large number of creditors.

3. a. An Internet company is likely to have higher indirect costs of financial distress because it has a lot of intangible assets, which lose much of their value if the company fails. On the other hand, most of the railroad company's assets are tangible. These assets have nearly the same value no matter who owns them.
   b. A pharmaceutical company is likely to have higher indirect costs of financial distress because its most valuable assets are its patents and R&D capability. These assets tend to lose value if the company fails. An automobile manufacturing

company's main assets are tangible assets that tend to retain their value no matter who owns them.

4. You should take a very risky investment project that offers a low profitability of a high p ayoff (at l east $1 b illion). If t his p roject fails, b ondholders w ill b ear t he loss. If this project succeeds, the company will fully pay off the bonds and pocket extra money for shareholders. This is a classic asset substitution problem that bondholders face.

5. The value of Anixter before the use of debt is:
$V_u = \text{EBIT} (1-T_c) / r_k$
$120 million = $20 million $(1-0.4) / r_k$
$r_k = $12 million / $120 million = 10\%$.

6. Without financial distress costs, the optimal level of debt is the maximum amount of debt that Anixter can use : $200 million.
The maximum value of Anixter is:
$V_L = V_u + T_cD$
$\quad = $120 million $+ (0.4)($200 million$) = $200 million.

7. With financial distress costs, the value of Anixter is:
$V_L = V_u + T_cD - PC$
where P = probability of financial distress
$\quad\quad$ C = present value of distress costs

D	$V_u + T_cD$	P	$PC = (P)\$80$	$V_L = V_U + T_CD - PC$
$20	$120	0	$0	$120
25	130	0	0	130
50	140	0.0125	1	139
75	150	0.0250	2	148
100	160	0.0625	5	155
125	170	0.1250	10	160
150	180	0.3125	25	155
200	200	0.7500	60	140

8. From the table above, the optimal debt level is $125 million.
The optimal debt-to-total asset ratio is:
$D / V = $125 / $160 = 78\%$.

9. The maximum value of Anixter when financial distress costs are included is $160 million.

10. The maximum value of Anixter without financial distress costs is $200 million. It corresponds with the maximum amount of debt. With financial distress cost, the maximum value of Anixter is $160 million. It corresponds with $125 million of debt.

14

DIVIDEND POLICY

CHAPTER SUMMARY

- Most corporations in the world pay regular cash dividends to shareholders. These dividends are generally a constant absolute amount rather than a constant fraction of the firm's earnings.

- Among developed countries, dividend payout ratios tend to be highest in British Commonwealth countries, whereas payouts are smaller in France and Italy.

- In the United States, corporations frequently repurchase shares on the open market rather than pay cash dividends.

- Stock splits and stock dividends are used by companies to reduce the per-share price.

- In a world without market imperfections, dividend policy is irrelevant because it does not affect the value of the firm.

- One theory of dividend policy assumes that dividend payments serve to reduce agency costs between corporate managers and outside investors by committing the firm to pay out excess profits, thereby preventing the managers from consuming the profits as perquisites. Most of the empirical evidence supports this agency cost model of dividends.

True or False Questions

T   F   1. Dividends and share repurchases are alternative means by which firms distribute cash to investors.

T   F   2. The percentage of firms paying dividends was four times greater in the 1950s than it is today

T   F   3. In the United States, as in most countries, shareholders have a legal right to receive dividends.

T   F   4. Most U.S. firms pay dividends quarterly, whereas corporations in other industrialized countries commonly pay dividends annually or semiannually.

T   F   5. The average ex-dividend day price drop in the United States is significantly less than 100 percent of the value of the dividend payment.

T   F   6. In the United States, laws prohibit a firm from paying more in dividends than its current earnings.

T   F   7. Empirical studies document that dividends and repurchases are complements in that companies paying high cash dividends also tend to be the companies most likely to repurchase their shares.

T   F   8. Companies with tangible assets as a large fraction of total value tend to have lower dividend payouts than companies with intangible assets as a large fraction of total market value.

T   F   9. Private companies rarely pay any dividends at all, whereas publicly traded companies pay out substantial fractions of their earnings as dividends.

T   F   10. Firms that increase dividends subsequently become less profitable and less risky, while the opposite happens to firms that cut dividends.

Multiple Choice Questions

1. Among 1,100 U.S. firms that paid dividends continuously from 1997 to 2001, the percent of theses firms that changed their dividend once per year is about:

    a. 13 percent.
    b. 20 percent.
    c. 24 percent.
    d. 30 percent.

2. The most popular dividend policy used by U.S. firms is:

    a. the constant payout ratio policy.
    b. the constant nominal payment policy.
    c. the low-regular-and-extra policy.
    d. the residual dividend policy.

3. Which of the following is not a method of distributing cash or securities to current shareholders?

    a. stock dividends
    b. seasoned equity offerings
    c. stock splits
    d. stock repurchases

4. Which of the following statements is false?

    a. Dividend and repurchases are complements in that companies paying high cash dividends also tend to be the companies most likely to repurchase their shares.
    b. Stock repurchases today are roughly twice as large in total value as ordinary cash dividends.
    c. Stock repurchases send a positive signal to investors in the marketplace that management believes that the stock is undervalued.
    d. U.S. firms have dramatically increased open-market repurchases of their own outstanding common stock in recent years.

5. Which of the following industries has the highest dividend payout ratio in the U.S.?

    a. pharmaceuticals
    b. alcoholic beverages and tobacco
    c. banking
    d. electric utilities

6. Adding personal taxes on dividend income to the frictionless market leads to the conclusion that:

    a. firms should retain all earnings.
    b. dividend policy is irrelevant.
    c. dividends are viewed as residuals from cash flow.
    d. dividend policy conveys significant new information.

7. In the United States, the market capitalization of firms that pay dividends relative to firms that do not is about:

    a. three times.
    b. five times.
    c. seven times.
    d. ten times.

8. An increase in which of the firm level variables tends to increase the dividend payout ratio?

    a. asset growth rate
    b. size of largest block holder
    c. number of individual shareholders
    d. positive NPV investment opportunities

9. An increase in which of these macroeconomic variables tends to reduce the dividend payout ratio?

    a. corporate governance power of institutional investors
    b. transaction costs of security issuance
    c. personal tax rates on capital gains income
    d. capital market relative to intermediated (bank) financing

10. Which of the following statements is false?

    a. Stock dividends are used by companies that wish to reduce the per-share price of their stock in the open market.
    b. In the United States, corporations frequently choose to repurchase shares on the open market rather than pay ordinary cash dividends.
    c. Empirical evidence indicates that stock prices fall on ex-dividend days by about 80% of the amount of the dividend.
    d. Firms that increase dividends subsequently become less profitable and less risky.

Questions and Problems

1. Sears follows a policy of paying out 55 percent of its net income as cash dividends to its shareholders each year. The company plans to do so again this year, during which Sears earns $110 million in net income. If the company has 30 million shares outstanding and pays dividends quarterly, what is the company's dividend per share each quarter?

2. Microsoft stock price is currently at $29 per share. The company announced recently that it will pay a quarterly dividend of $0.10 per share. What is the expected price of Microsoft on the ex-dividend date assuming that the stock price remains at $29 until the day before the ex-dividend date? Assume no personal taxes on dividend income received.

3. What are the differences between stock dividends and stock splits?

4. Johnson and Johnson stock price on March 13 was $80. In April, the firm paid a cash dividend of $1 per share. In May, J&J split its stock 2:1. In July, it raised the cash dividend to $1.25 per share. What is the firm's expected stock price after all these distributions? Assume no personal taxes on dividend income received.

5. DeVry distributes a 15% stock dividend. Before distributing the stock dividend, DeVry had 49 million shares. How many shares does the firm have after it makes the stock dividend distribution?

6. Kodak has paid out $15.4 million in dividends to its shareholders. The company earned $61.6 million. What is the firm's retention ratio?

7. Kroger retained $9.1 million from earnings of $11.2 million. What is the firm's payout ratio?

The following data apply to the next three problems:

Rouse Company is considering whether to use its $20 million accumulated cash to pay a cash dividend or to invest in the following projects:

Project	Initial Outlay	NPV
A	$10 million	$3 million
B	$7 million	$2 million
C	$4 million	$1 million

Rouse has 10 million shares outstanding and the share price is $50 (before the information on the projects is known).

8. Assume that Rouse cannot raise additional money. How much can Rouse invest?

9. What is the optimal amount of dividend paid by Rouse?

10. What will be the share price before Rouse pays dividends but after shareholders have information on the projects?

Solutions

True or False Questions

1. T   6. F
2. T   7. T
3. F   8. F
4. T   9. T
5. T   10. T

Multiple Choice Questions

1. D   6. A
2. B   7. D
3. B   8. C
4. B   9. A
5. B   10. C

Question and Problems

1. The annual total dividends are:
   55% x 100 million = $ 60.5 million.
   The quarterly dividends are:
   $ 60.5 million / 4 = $15.13 million.
   The quarterly dividends per share are:
   $15.13 million / 30 million = $0.504.

2. The expected price ex-dividend is:
   $29 - $0.1 = $28.90.

3. Although there is no economic difference between stock dividends and stock splits, the New York Stock Exchange defines any distribution of stock amounting to less that 25% of the shares investors hold as a stock dividend; any distribution of 25% or more as a stock split.

4. The expected stock price of J&J is:
   [($80 - $1)/2] - $1.25 = $38.25.

5. The number of shares of DeVry after the firm makes the stock dividend distribution is:
   (49 million)(1.15) = 56.35 million shares.

6. Kodak's payout ratio is:
   $15.4 million/$61.6 million = 25%.

Kodak's retention ratio is:
$$1 - 0.25 = 75\%.$$

7. The retention ratio of Kroger is:
$$\$9.1 \text{ million}/ \$11.2 \text{ million} = 81.25\%.$$
The firm's payout ratio is:
$$1 - 0.8125 = 18.75\%.$$

8. Rouse Company should invest $17 million in projects A and B. The firm does not have enough money left to accept project C.

9. The optimal amount of dividend is the leftover amount:
$$\$20 \text{ million} - \$17 \text{ million} = \$3 \text{ million}.$$

10. After shareholders know about the projects, the increase in Rouse stock price is:

$$(\$3 \text{ million} + \$2 \text{ million})/ 10 \text{ million} = \$0.5.$$
The new stock price is:
$$\$50 + \$0.5 = \$50.50.$$

15
ENTREPRENEURIAL FINANCE AND VENTURE CAPITAL

CHAPTER SUMMARY

- Entrepreneurial finance requires specialized financial management skills because entrepreneurial growth companies (EGCs) are unlike other private or publicly traded companies. EGCs must finance higher asset growth rates than other firms and must use external financial markets much more frequently.

- Venture capitalists (VCs) provide risk capital and managerial oversight to EGCs.

- U.S. venture capital investments are highly concentrated geographically and industrially. The most successful venture capital funds are almost always organized as limited partnerships and follow staged investment using convertible preferred stock.

- High growth in venture capital fund-raising and investment has occurred over the past in the United States, Western Europe, and in certain Asian countries, but not in Japan or in most developing countries.

True or False Questions

T   F 1. Entrepreneurial growth companies often achieve compound annual growth rates of 50 percent or more in sales and assets.

T   F 2. Once EGCs become publicly traded, they tend to rely on internal funding more than do older larger firms.

T   F 3. Personal equity financing and institutional loans constitute the two most important sources of start-up capital, accounting for about 60 percent of funds raised.

T   F 4. Pension funds typically account for 30-40 percent of all new money raised by institutional venture capital firms.

T   F 5. Firms located in New York consistently receive more venture backing than firms in any other state.

T   F 6. The earlier the development stage of the portfolio company, the higher must be the expected return on the venture capitalist's investment.

T   F 7. Professional venture capitalists typically demand compound annual investment returns in excess of 50 percent on start-up investments.

T   F 8. Most venture funds are organized and capitalized by private negotiation between the fund's sponsor and a well-established group of institutional investors.

T   F 9. Investments made by venture capital funds during the middle 1990s earned average compound annual returns of up to 20 percent.

T   F 10. Venture capitalists do not exit at the time of an IPO. Instead, they retain shares for several months or even years and then typically distribute shares back to the limited partners, rather than sell the shares on the open market.

Multiple Choice Questions

1. The compound annual growth rates in sales and assets typically achieved by entrepreneurial growth companies are:

    a. 30 percent or more.
    b. 40 percent or more.
    c. 50 percent or more.
    d. 60 percent or more.

2. The largest source of start-up capital for small companies is:

    a. personal equity.
    b. institutional loans.
    c. partnerships.
    d. loans from individuals.

3. Which of the following is not an institutional venture capital fund?

    a. venture capital limited partnerships
    b. corporate venture capital funds
    c. small business investment companies
    d. entrepreneurial finance companies

4. Which of the following has the largest market share of the venture capital industry?:

    a. venture capital limited partnerships
    b. corporate venture capital funds
    c. small business and investment companies
    d. financial venture capital funds

5. Annual venture capital investments in the United States increased steadily from 1991 until:

    a. 1999.
    b. 2000.
    c. 2001.
    d. 2002.

6. Which state receives the largest amount of venture capital investment?

    a. New York
    b. Texas
    c. California
    d. Massachusetts

7. Which stage of company development receives the most venture capital investments?

    a. later stage
    b. expansion
    c. start-up
    d. seed-stage

8. The security venture capitalists typically receive when they invest in a firm is:

    a. convertible preferred stock.
    b. common stock.
    c. convertible debt.
    d. non-convertible preferred stock.

9. Which stage of company development has the largest market share of European venture capital investment?

    a. start-up
    b. buyout
    c. expansion
    d. recapitalization

10. Which of the following countries has the smallest venture capital as a percentage of GDP?

    a. Canada
    b. Japan
    c. Israel
    d. United States

Questions and Problems

1. What is the difference between early-stage and later-stage venture capital investment? What percentage of venture capital has been allocated between the two in recent years?

2. Explain why venture capitalists use staged financing to minimize risk.

3. The venture capital fund, Oakmark, made a $13 million investment in Computer Technology Company four years ago and in return received 500,000 shares representing 15 percent of Computer Technology's equity. Computer Technology is now planning an initial public offering in which it will sell 5 million newly created shared for $30 per share. Oakmark decided to sell its shares alongside the newly created shares in Computer Technology's IPO. The investment banks will charge 8 percent underwriting fee, so both Oakmark and Computer Technology will receive 92 percent of the $30 per share offer price. Assume the IPO is successful, what annual rate of return will Oakmark have earned on its investment?

4. Suppose that 6 out of 10 investments made by a venture capital fund are a total loss, 2 break even, earning a 0 percent return. If the VC fund's expected return equals 40 percent, what rate of return must it earn on the two most successful deals to achieve a portfolio return equal to expectations?

5. An entrepreneur seeks $3 million from an angel capitalist. They agree that the entrepreneur's company is currently worth $10 million, and when the company goes public in an IPO in four years, it is expected to have a market capitalization of $60 million. The angel capitalist requires a 45 percent annual return on investment. What fraction of the firm will the angel capitalist receive in exchange for its $3 million investment?

6. An entrepreneur seeks $8 million from a VC fund. The entrepreneur and fund managers agree that the entrepreneur's company is currently worth $20 million and that the company's likely to be ready to go public in four years. At that time, the company is expected to have net income of $6.5 million, and comparable firms are expected to sell at a price/earnings ratio of 25. The venture capital fund managers require a 40 percent compound annual return on their investment. What fraction of the company will the fund receive in exchange for its $8 million investment?

The following data apply to the next four problems:

Acorn Fund made a $4 million investment in Internet Game Technology (IGT) five years ago and received 1 million shares of series A convertible preferred stock. Each of these shares in convertible into two shares of IGT common stock. Two years later, Acorn participated in a second round of financing for IGT and received 2 million shares of series B convertible preferred stock in exchange for $13 million investment. Each series B share is convertible into one share of IGT common stock. IGT is now planning an IPO, but before this the company will convert all its outstanding convertible preferred shares into common stock. After conversion, IGT will have 22 million common shares outstanding and will create another 3 million common shares for sale in the IPO. The underwriter handling IGT's initial offering expects to sell these shares for $30 each but has prohibited existing shareholders from selling any of their stock in the IPO. The underwriter will keep 8 percent of the offer as an underwriting discount. Assume that the IPO is successful and that IGT shares sell for $40 each immediately after the offering.

7. Calculate the total number of IGT shares that Acorn will own after the IPO. What fraction of IGT's total outstanding shares does this represent?

8. Using the IPO price for IGT shares, calculate the unrealized compound annual return Acorn earned on its original and subsequent investment in IGT stock.

9. Using the post-issue market price for IGT shares, calculate the unrealized compound annual return Acorn earned on its original and subsequent investment in IGT stock.

10. Now assume that the second round of IGT financing had been made under much less favorable conditions and that Acorn paid only $5 million instead of $13 million for the 2 million series B shares. Assuming that all the other features of IGT's IPO described above hold true and using the post-issue market price for IGT shares, calculate the unrealized compound annual return Acorn earned on this second investment in IGT stock.

SOLUTIONS

True or False Questions

1.	T	6.	T
2.	F	7.	T
3.	F	8.	T
4.	T	9.	F
5.	F	10.	T

Multiple Choice Questions

1.	C	6.	C
2.	B	7.	B
3.	D	8.	A
4.	A	9.	B
5.	C	10.	B

Questions and Problems

1. Earlier-stage financing, including start-up and seed-stage accounts for about a fifth of venture capital financing in 2002. A broader definition of early stage financing, including some expansion financing, would account for 35-50 percent of venture capital disbursements. Later-stage investments in more mature private companies account for about 18 percent of total venture capital investment in 2002. Their investments represent funding for marketing programs, major production plant expansions, and financing made in preparation for accessing the public capital market.

2. In staged financing, the venture capitals provide only a small percentage of the financing needed at first, just enough for the company to reach the next development stage. If the company succeeds, then the capitalists will provide more funding. Staged financing gives the venture capitalists an option to deny or delay additional financing, putting maximum risk on the entrepreneur.

3. The amount received by Oakmark for each IPO share is:

    92% x $30 = $27.60.
    The total amount received by Oakmark is:

    $27.60 x 500,000 = $13.8 million.
    Oakmark invested $3 million and received $13.8 million in 4 years. Solve for the annual rate of return:

    $3,000,000 = 13,800,000/ (1 + Return)^4$.
    Return = 47%.

4. 6 out of 10 earn - 100%, so expressed as a fraction of total portfolio:
    (0.6   x -1) = -0.60.
    2 out of 10 earn - 0%, so expressed as a fraction of total portfolio:
    (0.2 x 0) = 0.
    2 out of 10 earn must earn sufficient high returns (R) to make the following equation hold:

    $$0.40 = (0.2 \times R) + (0.6 \times -1) + (0.2 \times 0)$$
    $$= 0.2R - 0.6$$
    $$0.2R = 0.4 + 0.6 = 1.0$$
    R = 5.0, so these two investments must earn 500% each to make the portfolio average return of 40%.

5. Expected market value of the company in 4 years: $60 million. The required return on investment = 45%.
    The value of the angel capitalist's investment in 4 years is:
    $$3,000,000 \times (1.45)^4 = \$13,261,519.$$
    The fraction of equity received by the angel capitalist is:
    $13,261,519 / 60,000,000 = 22.1%.

6. Value of firm = Net income x P/E ratio
                   = $6.5 x 25 = $162.5 million.
    Required return on investment = 40%.
    The value of VC investment in 4 years:
    $$8,000,000 \times (1.4)^4 = \$30,732,800.$$
    The fraction of equity received by the VC fund is:
    $30,732,800 / $162,500,000= 18.91%.

7. Acorn will own 2 million common shares from its initial investment, and 2 million from its second round investment, a total of 4 million shares. There are 22 + 3 = 25 million shares in total, so Acorn will own 4/25 = 16% of IGT.

8. The first, five-year investment turned $4 million into $60 million (2 million shares x $30 = $60 million).

The return is:

$$4,000,000 = 60,000,000 / (1 + Return)^5$$

Return = 72%.

The second, three-year investment turned $13 million into $60 million (2 million shares x $30 = $60 million). The return is:

$$13,000,000 = 60,000,000 / (1 + Return)^3$$

Return = 67%.

9. Using the post-issue market price for IGT shares, the first, five-year investment turned $4 million into $80 million (2 million x $40 = $80 million). The return is:

$$4,000,000 = 80,000,000 / (1 + Return)^5$$

Return = 82%.

The second, three-year investment turned $13 million into $80 million. The return is:

$$13,000,000 = 80,000,000 / (1 + Return)^3$$

Return = 83%.

10. Assume that the second round investment was only $5 million with the same number of shares offered in return. Now, a $ 5 million investment turned into $80 million in three years. The return is:

$$5,000,000 = 80,000,000 / (1 + Return)^3$$

Return = 152%.

16

INVESTMENT BANKING AND THE PUBLIC SALE OF EQUITY SECURITIES

CHAPTER SUMMARY

- Companies wishing to raise new common stock equity must decide whether to sell stock to public investors through a general cash offering or to sell to existing stockholders via a rights offering.

- Common stock can be sold through private placements to accredited investors, or it can be sold to the public if the securities are registered with the SEC. A company's first public offering of common stock is called an initial public offering or IPO. The average IPO in the United States is under-priced by about 15 percent.

- Subsequent offerings of common stock are called seasoned equity offerings. The announcement of a seasoned equity issue tends to decrease the value of a company's common stock.

- Investment banks help companies sell new securities by underwriting security offerings. Underwriting a security offering involves three tasks: managing the offering, underwriting by purchasing the securities from the issuer at a fixed price, and selling the securities to investors.

True or False Questions

T   F 1. Corporate managers must enlist the help of an investment bank to sell the firm's securities.

T   F 2. The vast majority of equity sales are negotiated rather than competitive offers.

T   F 3. In a best-efforts arrangement, the investment bank purchases the shares from the issuing firm and resells them to investors.

T   F 4. The vast majority of U.S. initial public offerings have underwriting spreads of exactly 8 percent.

T   F 5. Investment banks charge higher spreads for initial public offerings than they do for seasoned equity offerings.

T   F 6. The Green Shoe option allows the lead underwriter and the selling group to sell up to an additional 15 percent more shares than originally planned.

T   F 7. Institutional investors generally receive 50-75 percent of shares offered in the typical IPOs.

T   F 8. A spin-off occurs when a parent company sells shares of a subsidiary corporation to the public through an initial public offering.

T   F 9. Seasoned equity offerings are rare for both U.S. and non-U.S. companies.

T   F 10. A share issue privatization involves the sale of shares in a state-owned company to private investors via a public capital market share offering.

Multiple Choice Questions

1. The vast majority of U.S. initial public offerings have underwriting spreads of:

    a. 5 percent.
    b. 6 percent.
    c. 7 percent.
    d. 8 percent.

2. Which of the following securities has the lowest underwriting spreads?

    a. convertible bonds
    b. preferred stock
    c. mortgage-backed securities
    d. seasoned equity offerings

3. The maximum percentage of additional shares that a lead underwriter can sell under the Green Shoe option is:

    a. 8 percent.
    b. 10 percent.
    c. 15 percent.
    d. 20 percent.

4.   What is the percentage represented by IPOs relative to all new common equity raised by American corporations each year?

    a. 20 percent
    b. 30 percent
    c. 50 percent
    d. 70 percent

5. Which of the following periods experienced the highest average first day return of initial public offerings?

   a. 1975-79
   b. 1980-89
   c. 1990-99
   d. 2000-01

6. What is the percentage of shares offered in the typical IPOs received by institutional investors?

   a. 30 percent
   b. 40 percent
   c. 60 percent
   d. 90 percent

7. Which of the following is not an advantage of an IPO to an American entrepreneur?

   a. personal wealth and liquidity
   b. the managerial costs of an IPO
   c. new capital for the company
   d. listed stock for use as a compensation vehicle

8. Which of the following is not a special type of IPOs:

   a. leveraged buyouts
   b. equity carve-outs
   c. tracking stocks
   d. spin-offs

9. Which of the following countries has the highest average first-day returns on IPOs?

   a. China
   b. Brazil
   c. Malaysia
   d. United States

10. The number of foreign companies that have shares traded in the United States in the form of sponsored and unsponsored ADRs is about:

   a. 900
   b. 1200
   c. 1500
   d. 1900

Questions and Problems

1. Why do investment banks require lockup agreements when they underwrite security offerings?

2. What is a rights offering? Explain the difference between a rights offering and other means of raising equity capital.

3. Differentiate between a best-efforts arrangement and a firm-commitment arrangement.

4. Data Technology Company (DTC) is going public for the first time. The company will sell 6 million shares at an offer price of $30 per share. The underwriter will charge a 7 percent underwriting fee, and the shares are expected to sell for $34 per share by the end of the first day's trading. Assume that the IPO is executed as expected.

   a. What is the initial return earned by investors who received allocated shares in the IPO?
   b. How much will DTC receive from this offering?
   c. What is the total cost of this issue to DTC?

5. Chicago Corporation needs to raise $30 million of new equity capital. Its common stock is currently selling for $51 per share. The investment banker requires an underwriting spread of 7 percent of the offering price, and the company's accounting and printing expenses associated with the seasoned offering are about $550,000. How many shares must the company sell to net $30 million?

6. Becker Company sold 10 million shares of common stock in a seasoned offering. The market price of the company's shares immediately before the offering was $23.75. The shares were offered to the public at $23.50, and the underwriting spread was 5 percent. The company's expenses associated with the offering were $2.9 million. How much new cash did Becker receive?

The following data apply to the next three problems.

A.G. Edwards specializes in underwriting new issues by medium-size firms. On a recent offering of 8 million shares of WMS at $15 per share, A.G. Edwards paid $110 million. The expenses incurred in the design and the distribution of the issue were $3.5 million

7. What profit or loss would A.G. Edwards incur if WMS were sold to the public at $15 per share?

8. What profit or loss would A.G. Edwards incur if WMS were sold to the public at an average price of $14.50 per share?

9. WMS is a cold IPO. A.G. Edwards has to cut the selling price to $12.50 per share. What is the loss incurred by A.G. Edwards?

10. You are a stockholder of Pfizer, which recently declared a rights offering. The current stock price with rights is $54 per share. The subscription price is $50 per share, and three rights are needed to purchase one share of common stock.

    a. Determine the theoretical value of the rights when the stock is trading with rights.
    b. Determine the theoretical value of the rights when the stock is trading ex rights.

SOLUTIONS

True or False Questions

1. F
2. T
3. F
4. F
5. T

6. F
7. T
8. F
9. T
10. T

Multiple Choice Questions

1. C
2. D
3. C
4. B
5. D

6. C
7. B
8. A
9. A
10. C

Questions and Problems

1. Investment banks require lockup agreements to ensure that company insiders will not profit from the superior private information about he company. Without the lockup agreement, an insider can sell shares immediately after the first-day run up of share prices.

2. In a rights offering, when a corporation issues additional shares, each shareholder is offered an option to buy a specified number of new shares at the subscription price within a period of time. If the corporation chooses to issue new stock to the public, they may either do so through a private placement or through an investment bank to reach a much wider group of domestic and international investors.

3. Under a best-efforts arrangement, the investment bank helps market the new issue but does not guarantee the issue or assume any risk. Under a firm-commitment arrangement, the investment underwrites the issue and guarantees the firm a certain amount per share regardless of market fluctuations.

4. a. In one day, investors allocated shares at $30 would have shares worth $34. Solving for return:

   $30 = 34 (1 + \text{return})$
   Return = 13.33%.

b. The proceed per share that DTC will receive is:

$30 (1 - .07) = $27.90
DTC will receive $27.90 x 5 million = $139.5 million.

c. The total cost of the issue is:
($34 - $27.90) x 5 million = $30.5 million.

5. The Chicago Corporation needs to raise $30,000,000 + $550,000 = $30,550,000
The net proceed per share to the company is
$51 (1 – 0.07) = $47.43.
The number of shares the company must sell is:
$30,550,000 / $47.43 = 644,108 shares.

6. The proceed per share to the company is:
$23.50 (1 – 0.05) = 22.325.
The new cash received by Becker is:
(22.325 x 6 million) - $2.9 million = $131.05 million.

7. The profit made by A.G. Edwards is:
($15)(8 million) - $110 million - $3.5 million = $6.5 million.

8. The profit made by A.G. Edwards is;
($14.5) (8 million) - $110 million -$3.5 million = $2.5 million.

9. The loss incurred by A.G. Edwards is:
($12.5)(8 million) - $110 million - $3.5 million = -$13.5 million.

10. a. The theoretical value of a right where the stock is trading with rights is:
$Rw = (Mw – S) / (N+1) = ($54 - $50)/4 = 1.

b. The theoretical value of a right when the stock is trading ex rights is:
$Re = (Me – S) / N = [($54 - $1) - $50]/3 = 1.

17
LONG-TERM DEBT AND LEASING

Chapter Summary

- Long-term debt and leasing are important sources of capital for companies. Long-term debt can be term loans or bonds. The conditions of a term loan typically has several positive and negative covenants that the borrower must not violate.

- The conditions of a bond are specified in the bond indenture. This legal agreement is highly detailed and not easily modified, because bonds are held by many individual investors.

- Syndicated loans are large credits arranged by a syndicate of commercial banks for a single borrower.

- Leasing serves as an alternative to borrowing funds to buy an asset. Operating leases need not be shown on a firm's balance sheet, whereas capital lease obligations must be shown.

True or False Questions

T   F 1. The total value of syndicated loans funded by multiple banks exceeds that of single-lender term loans by a wide margin.

T   F 2. The majority of both term loans and syndicated loans are fixed-rate issues.

T   F 3. An example of a negative covenant is that the borrower is required to maintain a minimum level of net working capital.

T   F 4. Generally, long-term loans have higher interest rates than short-term loans.

T   F 5. A term loan is made by a financial institution to a business and has an initial maturity from 10 to 20 years.

T   F 6. To issue a callable bond, the firm must pay a higher interest rate than that of noncallable bonds of equal risk.

T   F 7. Bonds rated Baa or lower by Moody's are called high-yield bonds or junk bonds.

T   F 8. A foreign bond is a bond issued by an international borrower and sold to investors in countries with currencies other than the currency in which the bond is denominated.

T   F 9. The lessor uses the underlying asset and makes regular payments to the lessee, who retains ownership of the asset.

T   F 10. Operating leases are commonly used for leasing land, buildings, and large pieces of equipment.

Multiple Choice Questions

1.   Which of the following is a private debt?

    a. mortgage bonds
    b. equipment trust certificates
    c. debentures
    d. syndicated loans

2.   Which of the following is not commonly used by lessors of financial leases?

    a. computer systems
    b. land
    c. large pieces of equipment
    d. buildings

3.   Which of the following bonds is unsecured?

    a. income bonds
    b. collateral trust bonds
    c. limited open-end mortgage bonds
    d. equipment trust certificates

4.   Bonds that received investment-grade ratings when they were first issued but later fell to junk status are called:

    a. income bonds
    b. fallen angels
    c. subordinated debentures
    d. putable bonds

5.   Which of the following is not an advantage of leasing?

    a. A lease does not have a stated interest cost.
    b. Leasing allows the lessee, in effect, to depreciate land.
    c. Leasing provides 100 percent financing.
    d. A lessee avoids many of the restrictive covenants that are usually included as part of a long-term loan.

6. Which of the following leases typically does not appear on the balance sheet of the lessee?

    a. land leases
    b. building leases
    c. automobile leases
    d. large equipment leases

7. Which of the following loans are typically arranged to finance toll roads and airports?

    a. collateral trust bonds
    b. project finance loans
    c. equipment trust certificates
    d. eurocurrency loans

8. The term that requires the issuing firm to retire some portion of its bonds every year is called the:

    a. sinking fund provision
    b. call provision
    c. indenture
    d. positive covenant

9. High-yield bonds or junk bonds are rated:
    a. Ba or below by Moody's.
    b. Baa or below by Moody's.
    c. BBB or below by Standard and Poor's.
    d. A or below by Standard and Poor's.

10. A bond denominated in one currency, such as the British pound, but traded simultaneously in a number countries is called a:
    a. foreign bond
    b. bearer bond
    c. bulldog bond
    d. Eurobond

Questions and Problems

1. Why do long-term debt agreements normally include restrictive covenants?

The following data apply to the next three questions.

Bond	Annual Coupon Rate	Maturity	Rating	Call Price
GE	5%	25 years	AAA	105% of par
ITT	7%	30 years	A	107% of par
Tyco	9%	25 years	BBB	108% of par
AT&T	6%	30 years	AA	105% of par
AMR	10%	20 years	BB	110% of par

2. Which bond has the highest call risk? Why?

3. Which bond is a high-yield or junk bond?

4. If interest rate increases by 0.25%, which bond will have the largest price decrease? Explain.

5. Callable and convertible bonds are bonds with embedded options.

   a. What option is embedded in a callable bond? Who owns the option?
   b. What option is embedded in a convertible bond? Who owns the option?

6. A company that issues income bonds must pay interest on these bonds only when its income is positive. Is an income bonds more like debt or equity?

7. For each of the callable bond in the table, calculate the after-tax cost of calling the issue. Each bond has $1,000 par value, and various issue sizes and a call prices are shown in the table. The firm is in the 35 percent tax bracket.

Bond	Size of Issue	Call Price
GM	50,000 bonds	$1,040
FRE	40,000	1,030
IGT	30,000	1,045
IBM	90,000	1,050
Intel	60,000	1,060

8. Given the lease payments and terms shown in the following table, calculate the yearly after-tax cash outflows for each firm, assuming that lease payments are made at the beginning of each year and that the firm is in the 35 percent tax bracket. Assume that no purchase option exists.

Firm	Annual Lease Payment	Term of Lease
Cisco	$950,000	6 years
Ryder	830,000	12
CSX	1,210,000	20
Wal-Mart	1,560,000	8

9. Given the lease payments, terms remaining until the leases expire, and discount rates shown in the following table, calculate the capitalized value of each lease, assuming that lease payments are made annually at the beginning of each year.

Firm	Lease Payment	Remaining Terms	Discount Rate
DuPont	$9,950,000	12 years	9%
3M	7,820,000	10	12%
Boeing	12,560,000	20	10
Pfizer	5,630,000	4	8

10. The principal, coupon interest rate, and interest overlap period are shown in the following table for four bonds.

Bond	Principle	Coupon Interest Rate	Interest Overlap Period
Sears	$35,000,000	7%	3 months
Wendy's	15,000,000	8	2
Dana	9,000,000	6.5	6
Merck	20,000,000	5.5	1

a. Calculate the dollar amount of interest that must be paid for each bond during the interest overlap period.

b. Calculate the after-tax cost of overlapping interest for each bond if the firm is in the 40 percent tax bracket.

SOLUTIONS

True or False Questions

1. T
2. F
3. F
4. T
5. F

6. T
7. F
8. F
9. F
10. T

Multiple Choice Questions

1. D
2. A
3. A
4. B
5. A

6. C
7. B
8. A
9. A
10. D

Questions and Problems

1. Restrictive covenants protect bondholders, reduce bondholder-stockholder conflict and lower the cost of debt because of those protections.

2. The AT&T bond has the highest call risk because it has the longest time to maturity and the lowest call price

3. The AMR bond is a junk bond because its rating is BB.

4. The AT&T bond will have the largest price decrease because it has the longest time to maturity and a lower coupon rate than the ITT bond, which has the same time to maturity.

5. a. Embedded in a callable bond is a call option that allows the issuing firm to retire the bond at a specified price written a period of time. The issuing firm owns the option.
   b. Embedded in a convertible bond is an option that allows the bondholder to convert the bond to a fixed number of shares of the common stock within a specified period. The bondholder owns the option.

6. An income bond has some of the characteristics of debt and equity. Income bondholders have superior claim on cash flows relative to preferred and common stockholders. The payments are tax-deductible to the company. These are characteristics of debt. However, the bondholder claim is variable because the

company is not required to make these payments periodically. This is a characteristic of equity.

7. Call premium per bond = Call price - Par Value
   Total Call premium = Call premium per bond x Number of bonds
   After-tax cost of calling bond issue = Total call premium

Bond	Call premium per bond	Total call premium	After-tax cost of calling issue
GM	$40	$2,000,000	$1,300,000
FRE	30	1,200,000	780,000
IGT	45	1,350,000	877,500
IBM	50	4,500,000	2,925,000
Intel	60	3,600,000	2,340,000

8. The yearly after-tax cash flows are the lease payment x (1- tax rate)

Firm	Lease Payment	After-tax cash flow
Cisco	$ 950,000	$ 617,500
Ryder	830,000	539,500
CSX	1,210,000	786,500
Wal-Mart	1,560,000	1,014,000

9. The capitalized value of each lease is the present value of an annuity (lease payment) discounted at the given discount rate for the remaining term of the leases.

Firm	Lease Payment	Remaining Term	Discount Rate	Capitalized Value
DuPont	$9,950,000	12 years	9%	$71,251,950
3M	7,820,000	10	12	44,183,000
Boeing	12,560,000	20	10	106,935,840
Pfizer	5,630,000	4	8	18,646,560

10. Interest payable during overlap = Coupon rate x Principal x (Months overlap / 12)

   After-tax cost of overlapping interest = Interest during overlap period x (1 - tax rate)

Bond	Calculation of interest payable during overlap period	Interest payable during overlap	After-tax cost of overlapping interest
Sears	$35,000,000 x 0.07 x 3/12	$612,500	$ 367,500
Wendy	15,000,000 x 0.08 x 2/12	200,000	120,000
Dana	9,000,000 x 0.065 x 6/12	292,500	175,500
Merck	20,000,000 x 0.055 x 1/12	91,667	55,000

OPTIONS BASICS

Chapter Summary

- Options are contracts that allow the buyer the right to buy or sell stock at a fixed price on or before a certain date.

- Call options grant the right to buy shares. Put options grant the right to sell shares.

- Payoff diagrams show the value of options on the expiration date.

- Put-call parity establishes a link between the market prices of calls, puts, shares, and bonds, provided certain conditions hold.

- An increase in the volatility of the underlying asset increases the values of calls and puts.

- The binomial option-pricing model and the risk-neutral method can calculate option prices with a minimum set of assumptions.

True or False Questions

T   F   1. Put options obligate the holder to sell stock at a fixed price on or before a certain date.

T   F   2. In many of the foreign markets, trading in equity derivatives exceeds the volume of trading in the underlying stocks.

T   F   3. A put option is in the money if the option's strike price is less than the current stock price.

T   F   4. When the price of a stock moves, the dollar change of the stock is generally more than the dollar change of the option price, but the percentage change in the option price is much greater than the percentage change in the stock price.

T   F   5. A naked call occurs when an investor sells a call option on a stock while owning that underlying stock

T   F   6. The put-call parity implies that investors can create a synthetic put by purchasing a bond and a call while simultaneously short-selling the stock.

T   F 7. Call and put prices decrease when the difference between the underlying stock
          and the exercise price decreases.

T   F 8. Whether investors are risk averse or risk neutral, the binomial model's
          calculations are the same.

T   F 9. An increase in the volatility of the underlying asset increases the value of call
          and decreases the value of puts.

T   F 10. Options provide a real economic benefit to society and are not simply a form of
          legalized gambling.

Multiple Choice Questions

1. Which of the following is not a derivative security?

    a. futures contracts
    b. swaps
    c. preferred stock
    d. put options

2. According to the put-call parity, the sum of the call value and the present value of the
   strike price minus the stock price is equal to the:

    a. put price.
    b. intrinsic value.
    c. time value.
    d. bond price.

3. An investor who is optimistic about a stock price should:

    a. buy a put.
    b. buy the stock and sell a call.
    c. sell a call.
    d. sell a put.

4. Which of the following strategies is a hedge?

    a. buy the stock and sell a put
    b. buy the stock and sell a call
    c. sell a put
    d. buy a call

5. Which of the following decreases the value of a call?

    a. The volatility of the underlying stock increases.
    b. The difference between the underlying stock price and the exercise price decreases.
    c. The time to maturity increases.
    d. The exercise price of the call decreases.

6. The value of a put increases when:

    a. its exercise price increases.
    b. the difference between the underlying stock and the exercise price increases.
    c. the volatility of the underlying stock decreases.
    d. there is less time left before expiration

7. Which of the following strategies is the riskiest?

    a. buy a put
    b. buy the stock and sell a call
    c. buy a straddle
    d. sell a call

8. Which of the following strategies offers the highest potential payoff?

    a. buy a put
    b. buy a call
    c. short a stock
    d. short a straddle

9. Which of the following countries does not rank among the world's top-10 equity derivative markets in terms of annual trading volume?

    a. Brazil
    b. Germany
    c. Canada
    d. France

10. When the price of a stock moves, the dollar change of the stock is _____ than the dollar change of the option price, and the percentage change in the option price is _____ than the percentage change in the stock price.

    a. more, more
    b. less, less
    c. more, less
    d. less, more

Questions and Problems

1. A put option with a strike price of $70 was priced at 43.50. At expiration, the underlying stock is selling for $74.50. If you wrote this put $3.50, what would be your profit or loss at expiration?

2. Suppose you buy a DuPont put for $3, which expires in two months with a strike price of $65. DuPont is currently trading at $66.75. If the stock price falls to $60 in two months, what is your rate of return on your put option?

3. Suppose the stock price of AT&T is $62, and the three-month call price is $2.50 with a strike price of $65. If AT&T stock rises to $69 in three months, what is your rate of return on your call?

4. Suppose the stock price of HBO is $48, and the two-month call price is $3 with a strike price of $50. You hedge by buying HBO stock at $48 and sell the call. If HBO stock rises to $54 in two months, what is the profit or loss on your strategy?

5. Suppose the stock price of Costco is $54, and the three-month call price is $4 with a strike price of $55. You hedge by buying Costco stock at $54 and sell the call. If Costco stock falls to $48 in three months, what is the profit or loss of your strategy?

6. Suppose you write a naked call option on Johnson Controls stock at a strike price of $80 for a premium of $4.50. What will you gain or lose on the call and what will the break-even point be if at option expiration date the stock closes at $88?

7. Assume you buy a put on General Motors at a strike price of $50 for $3.50 when GM is selling at $49 a share. If the stock closes at $58.75 at the expiration date, what will be the value of the put option?

8. At expiration, a 3M call with a strike price of $100 has a price of $7. 3M stock is selling for $110.

    a. How do you take advantage of this pricing?
    b. At what price must the call sell to prevent arbitrage?
    c. What transaction would you make if the 3M call had a price of $12 at the expiration date?

9. Assume you sell short 100 shares of General Dynamics at $68 in May. You buy a July $70 call for $2.50 to protect yourself from an increase in stock price. If General Dynamics closes at $80 at the expiration date of the call, what is your gain or loss?

10. A call expires in two months and has a strike price of $50. The underlying stock is worth $52 today. In two months, the stock may increase by $5 or decrease by $4. The risk-free rate is 3 percent per year. Use the binomial option-pricing model to value the call price.

SOLUTIONS

True or False Questions

1. F
2. T
3. F
4. T
5. F

6. T
7. F
8. T
9. F
10. T

Multiple Choice Questions

1. C
2. A
3. D
4. B
5. B

6. A
7. D
8. B
9. C
10. A

Questions and Problems

1. You make a profit of $3.50 at expiration because the put will not be exercised, i.e., the put is out of the money.

2. The value of the put at expiration is:
         $65-$60 = $5.

    Your rate of return on the put is:
         ($5-$3)/$3 = 66.67%.

3. The value of the AT&T call at expiration is:
         $69-$65 = $4.
    Your rate of return on the AT&T call is:
         ($4-$2.50)/$2.50 = 60%.

4. If HBO stock rises to $54, the call will be exercised. You receive only $50 for the stock, with a capital gain of $2. You keep the call premium of $3. Therefore, your total profit from the strategy is $5.

5. If Costco stock falls to $8, the call will not be exercised. You lose $6 on the stock ($48 - $54) but you keep the $4 premium of the call. Therefore the loss on this strategy is $2. If you did not hedge, the loss would have been $6.

6. You have to buy the stock at $88 to deliver and receive the strike price of $80. The loss on the call is -$8+$4.50 = -$3.50. The break - even point is $80 + $ 4.50 = $84.50.

7. The value of the put is zero because GM stock price closes above the strike price of $50 at the expiration date.

8. a. Because the call is underpriced, you would:

Transaction	Cash Flow
Buy 3M call	-$7
Exercise the call	-$100
Sell the stock	+110
Net cash flow	+$3

You made an arbitrage profit of $3.

b. The call price of $10 would prevent any arbitrage opportunity.

c. Because the call is overpriced, you would:

Transaction	Cash Flow
Sell 3M call	+$12
Buy the share	-$110
Initial cash flow:	-$98

The call buyer must immediately exercise the call because it is in-the-money at expiration.

Transaction	Cash Flow
Deliver shares	$0
Collect strike price	+$100
Total net cash flow	+2
You made an arbitrage profit of	$2.

9. The overall loss consists of:
The loss of the stock position: $68-$80 = ($12.00)
The gain of the call position: $10 - $2.50 = $7.50
                                            ($4.50)

10.   <u>Cash Flow in 2 months</u>

	<u>Cash Flow in 2 months</u>	
Share	Price Up	Price Down
Call option	$57	$48
Total	57 + 7h	48 + 0h

Set the two equal and solve for h, the hedge ratio:

57 + 7h = 48

h = -1.29 call options.

If you buy a share and sell 1.29 call options, you will have the same payoff whether the price goes up or down, an asset with a value of $48. The present value of $48, discounted at .03 x 2/12 = 0.005 for two months, is $48/1.005 = $47.76.

Solving for h:

52-1.29 C = 47.76

-1.29 C = -4.42

C= $3.29.

19

BLACK AND SCHOLES AND BEYOND

Chapter Summary

- The Black and Scholes option-pricing equation requires five inputs: the stock price, the strike price, the risk-free rate, the time to expiration, and the underlying asset's volatility. Of the five inputs, only volatility is an unknown, which must be estimated.

- Analysts can use the Black and Scholes formula to value a European call on a stock that pays no dividends.

- When a firm borrows money, both its debt and equity have option-like characteristics.

- Warrants are similar to call options but pricing warrants requires an adjustment to the Black and Scholes model to account for dilution.

- Convertible securities combine characteristics of bonds with call options.

- Real options can be valued using the binomial or the Black and Scholes model.

True or False Questions

T   F 1. The option's delta equals the value $N(d2)$ from the Black and Scholes equation.

T   F 2. In the Black and Scholes model, the ratio $1 / N(d1)$ is equivalent to the hedge ratio from the binomial model.

T   F 3. The Black and Scholes model was originally conceived to price American call option on an underlying stock that paid no dividends.

T   F 4. Call and put options always sell for more than their intrinsic value.

T   F 5. The Black and Scholes model requires five inputs that can all be readily observed in the market.

T   F 6. Empirical tests of Black and Scholes model find that options with the same underlying stock have the same implied volatilities.

T   F 7. Empirical studies document that option prices generated by Black and Scholes model are close to actual market prices for at-the-money options, but pricing error are more substantial for out-of-the-money options.

T   F 8. A convertible bond is essentially a corporate bond with an attached call or warrant.

T   F 9. LYONs (liquid-yield option notes) are zero-coupon bonds that automatically convert to common shares at a future date.

T   F 10. NPV calculations often understate the value of an investment, but pricing corporate real options using decision trees leads to overvaluation errors.

Multiple Choice Questions

1. Which of the following is not an input of the Black and Scholes equation:

    a. the stock price
    b. the time to expiration
    c. the expected return on the underlying stock
    d. the volatility of the underlying stock

2. Which of the following is equivalent to the hedge ratio from the binomial model:

    a. N(d1).
    b. N(d2).
    c. 1/N(d1).
    d. 1/N(d2).

3. When a call option's far out-of-the-money, the option's delta is:

    a. close to zero.
    b. almost 1.0.
    c. close to 0.5.
    d. equivalent to the hedge ratio.

4. Which of the following firms is the top dealer in over the counter derivatives?

    a. Goldman Sachs
    b. Citigroup
    c. Morgan Stanley
    d. Merrill Lynch

5. Which of the following statements about warrants is false?

a. Warrants are issued by firms.
b. Warrants are often issued with expiration dates several months in the future.
c. When investors exercise warrants, the number of outstanding shares increases.
d. Firms frequently attach warrants to bonds

6. The number of shares that bondholders will receive if they convert is called the:

   a. conversion value.
   b. conversion premium.
   c. conversion price.
   d. conversion ratio.

7. Convertibles that automatically convert to shares at a future date are called:

   a. Lyons (liquid yield option notes).
   b. death spiral.
   c. DECS (debt exchangeable for common shares).
   d. forced convertible bond.

8. In the Black and Scholes model, the option value does not depend on:

   a. the expected rate of return on the stock.
   b. the risk-free rate.
   c. the variance of the stock.
   d. the strike price.

9. In the Black and Scholes model, if the volatility of the stock increases:

   a. the value of a call would increase, but the value of a put would decrease.
   b. both the value of a call and a put would decrease.
   c. both the value of a call and a put would increase.
   d. the value of a call would decrease, but the value of a put would increase.

10. In the Black and Scholes model, the value of a call decreases with an increase in:

   a. the strike price.
   b. the time to maturity.
   c. the risk-free rate.
   d. the stock price.

Questions and Problems

1. Sun Microsystems issues a convertible bond yielding 4%. The conversion ratio is 50. The bond sells at par value of $1,000.

a. What is the conversion price?
b. If the current stock price is $15, what is the conversion value of the bond?
c. What is the conversion premium?

2. Determine the premium of a bond that is convertible into 20 shares of common stock trading at $42.25 per share. The bond is selling at $1,000 and has a straight debt value of $844.

3. Use the Black and Scholes model to value a call with a strike price of $20 and an expiration date in three months. The underlying stock sells for $20 and has a standard deviation of 16 percent, and the risk-free rate is 12 percent.

4. Use the Black and Scholes model to value a call with a strike price of $40 and an expiration date in six months. The underlying stock sells for $42 and has a standard deviation of 20 percent per year, and the risk-free rate is 10 percent.

5. Use the information in problem 4, calculate the value of a put with a strike price of $40.

The following data apply to problems 6 through 10

It is July 1 and Lee stock is at $110. Assume that the stock will pay no dividends between now and the end of November. Premiums for Lee options are as follows:

Stock Price	Strike Price	Calls		Puts	
		Aug.	Nov.	Aug.	Nov.
$110	$105	$8.50	$13.50	$3.00	$6.75
110	110	5.25	10.25	4.75	9.00
110	115	3.50	8.00	7.25	11.75

Jim Smith is considering trading some of the Lee calls if they are properly priced. He asked you to use the Black-Scholes model to calculate the price of Lee calls, given the following information:

Risk-free rate = 4% annualized

Time to expiration for the November option = 142 days

Estimated daily variance of the stock = 0.00040

6. Using the Black and Scholes model, calculate the price of the November 110 call. Does the model suggest that the call is undervalued or overvalued?

7. In checking other data, you discover that other traders are using a variance estimate of 0.00034. Recalculate the price of the November 110 call using this variance.

8. Making calculations using the daily variance of 0.0004, what are the values of the deltas of the November 105 call and the November 115 call?

9. How many shares of stock would you use to create a riskless arbitrage portfolio for the November 105 call? For the November 115 call?

10.   Using the Black and Scholes model, calculate the price for the November 110 put.

SOLUTIONS

True or False Questions

1. F	6. F
2. T	7. T
3. F	8. T
4. F	9. F
5. F	10. T

Multiple Choice Questions

1. C	6. D
2. C	7. C
3. A	8. A
4. B	9. C
5. B	10. A

Questions and Problems

1. a. The conversion price is:
        $1,000 / 50 = $20.
    b. The conversion value of the bond is:
        $15 x 50 = $750.
    c. The conversion premium is:
        $1,000 - $750 = $250.

2. The bond's conversion value is greater than the straight debt value. Therefore, the premium is:
    $1,000 − (45.25)(20) = $1,000 - $905 = $95.

3. The values of d1, and d2 are:

    $$d_1 = \frac{\ln(20/20) + [0.12 + (0.16/2)](0.25)}{0.4(0.5)}$$

    $$= (0+0.05)/0.2 = 0.25.$$

    $$d_2 = d_1 - 0.4(0.25)^{.5} = 0.25 - 0.2 = 0.05.$$

    $N(d_1) = N(0.25) = 0.5987.$
    $N(d_2) = N(0.05) = 0.5199.$

    The value of the call is:

    $$C = 20[N(d_1)] - 20e^{-(0.12)(0.25)}[N(d_2)]$$
    $$= 20(0.5987) - 19.41(0.5199)$$
    $$= 11.97 - 10.09 = \$1.88.$$

4. The values of d_1 and d_2 are:

$$d_1 = \frac{\ln(42/40) + (0.1 + 0.2^2/2)(0.5)}{0.2(0.5)^{.5}}$$
$$= 0.7693.$$

$$d_2 = \frac{\ln(42/40) + (0.1 - 0.2^2/2)(0.5)}{0.2(0.5)^{.5}}$$
$$= 0.6278.$$

$$N(d_1) = N(0.7693) = 0.7791$$
$$N(d_2) = N(0.6278) = 0.7349$$

The value of the call is:
$$C = 42N(0.7693) - 40e^{-(0.1)(0.5)}N(0.6278)$$
$$= 42\,(0.7791) - 38.049\,(0.7349) = \$4.76.$$

5. $d_1 = 0.7693$, $N\,(-0.7693) = 0.2209$

$d_2 = 0.6278$, $N\,(-0.6278) = 0.2651$

The value of the put is:
$$P = 38.049\,N(-0.6278) - 42\,N(-0.7693)$$
$$= 38.049(0.2651) - 42\,(0.2209)$$
$$= \$0.81.$$

6. The Black Scholes equation to calculate call values is:

$$C = N(d_1)S - X(e^{-rt})N(d_2)$$

$$d_1 = \frac{\ln(S/X) + (r + o^2/2)T}{o(T)^{.5}}$$

$$d_2 = d_1 - o(T)^{.5}$$

$$d_1 = \frac{\ln(110/110) + (0.04/365 + 0.0004/2)142}{(0.0004)^{.5}(142)^{.5}} = \frac{0.0440}{0.2383} = 0.1845.$$

$$d_2 = 0.1845 - (0.0004)^{.5}(142)^{.5} = -0.0539.$$

$$C = N(0.1845)110 - 110(e^{-0.00011(142)})N(-0.0539)$$
$$C = 0.5714(110) - 110(0.9845)(0.4792) = \$10.96.$$

The market price is \$10.25, suggesting the November 110 call is undervalued.

7. Using a variance estimate of 0.00034, the November 110 call's value is:

$$d_1 = \frac{\ln(110/110 \ \ + (0.04/365 + 0.00034/2)142}{(0.00034)^{.5}(142)^{.5}} = \frac{0.0397}{0.2197} = 0.1807$$

$$d_2 = 0.1907 - (0.00034)^{.5}(142)^{.5} = -0.0390$$

$$C = N(0.1807)110 - 110(e^{-0.00011)(142)})N(-0.0390)$$
$$C = 0.5659(110) - 110(0.9845)(0.4848) = \$9.75.$$

8. The delta of the call is N(d1), for the November 105 call, the delta is:
$$d_1 = = [\ln(110/105 + (0.04/365 + 0.0004/2)142]/0.2383 = 0.3797$$
$$N(d_1) = 0.648.$$
For the November 115 call, the delta is:
$$d_1 = [\ln(110/115 + (0.04/365 + 0.0004/2)142]/0.2383 = -0.0021$$
$$N(d_1) = 0.492.$$

9. For the November 105 call: 1/0.648 = 1.54 shares per option.

For the November 115 call: 1/0.492 = 2.03 shares per option.

10. The Black and Scholes equation to calculate put value is:

$$P = -N(-d_1)S + X(e^{-rt})N(-d_2)$$

For the November 110 put:
$$-d_1 = -0.1845 \text{ (from problem 6)}$$
$$-d_2 = 0.0539 \text{ (from problem 6)}$$
$$P = -0.4286(110) + 110(0.9845)(0.5209) = \$9.26.$$

20

INTERNATIONAL FINANCIAL MANAGEMENT

Chapter Summary

- Multinational corporations (MNCs) dominate international trade and investment today. MNCs tend to be the most dynamic and successful firms in the industry.

- Any company that exports goods and services is exposed to exchange rate risk. Importers can face similar risks, though this is less common because sales are usually denominated in the customer's currency. Several hedging techniques have developed to reduce this risk; the most common is hedging with forward contracts.

- The total volume of foreign direct investment (FDI) increased significantly in the 1990s. The equity participation on the part of an MNC can be quite large, up to 100 percent. By nature, FDI involves equity participation, managerial control, and day-to-day operational activities on the part of MNCs.

- MNCs must pay attention to their management of cash, accounts receivable, and other short-term assets, given the potential damage of loss from exchange rate fluctuations.

True or False Questions

1. T F Since the mid-1970, the major currencies of the world have had a fixed exchange rate with the U.S. dollar

2. T F In a currency board arrangement, a national currency continues to circulate, but every unit of the currency is fully backed by government holdings of another currency, usually the U.S. dollar.

3. T F Whenever one currency buys more of another on the forward market than it does on the spot market, then the first currency trades at a forward premium.

4. T F The foreign exchange market is the world's largest financial market.

5. T F The forward-spot parity is strongly supported by empirical results.

6. T F If inflation is higher in one country than another, then the currency of the country with higher inflation will appreciate.

7. T   F   Purchasing power parity does a good job of explaining both long-run and short-run movements in currencies.

8. T   F   When a nation's currency trades at a forward premium, risk-free interest rates in that country should be lower than they are abroad.

9. T   F   The exchange rate risk can be eliminated by hedging with financial contracts.

10. T   F   Foreign direct investment is the transfer by a mutinational firm of financial, managerial, and technical assets from its home country to a host company.

Multiple Choice Questions

1. Which of the following exchange rate systems is used by most countries in the world?

   a. a floating exchange rate system
   b. a fixed exchange rate system
   c. a managed floating rate system
   d. a currency board arrangement

2. The exchange rate that applies to currency trades that occur in the future is called the:

   a. spot exchange rate.
   b. forward premium.
   c. forward discount.
   d. forward exchange rate.

3. From 1984 to 1996, which of the following countries has the highest inflation rate?

   a. Germany
   b. United States
   c. France
   d. Japan

4. Which of the following is not a parity condition that influences relative currency values?

   a. real interest ratc parity
   b. forward-futures parity
   c. purchasing power parity
   d. interest rate parity

5. Which of the following is not a hedging tool for exchange rate risk?

    a. futures contracts
    b. options
    c. currency swaps
    d. common stock

6. Which of the following parity is an extension of the law of one price?

    a. purchasing power parity
    b. interest rate parity
    c. forward-spot parity
    d. real interest rate parity

7. The model that offers insights into the causes of currency movements is the:

    a. capital asset pricing model.
    b. asset market model.
    c. arbitrage pricing model.
    d. Black and Scholes model.

8. Which of the following exchange rate systems is the least popular?

    a. a managed floating rate system
    b. a currency board arrangement
    c. a floating exchange rate system
    d. a fixed exchange rate system

9. Which of the following statements is false?

    a. Multinational corporations are companies that operate in many countries around the world.
    b. For the past 30 years, the exchange rates of major currencies have fluctuated daily.
    c. The foreign exchange market is not a physical market, but a global telecommunications market.
    d. Empirical studies find that the forward exchange rate provides a reliable forecast of future spot rates.

10. Which of the following statements is true?

    a. When a nation's currency trades at a forward discount, risk-free interest rates in that country should be lower than they are abroad.
    b. Changes in the nominal exchange rate are those that exactly mirror changes in relative inflation rates between two countries whereas changes in the real exchange rate measure changes in the purchasing power of a currency.
    c. The interest rate parity is also referred to as the Fisher effect.
    d. An example of macro political risk is the nationalization of the assets of international oil companies.

Questions and Problems

1. What role does the triangular arbitrage play in the currency markets?

2. Does interest rate parity imply that interest rates are the same in all countries?

3. On May 2, 2003, the Euro-U.S. dollar exchange rate was 0.9264 Euro/$ ($1.0795 / Euro). On July 10, 2003, the exchange rate was 0.878 Euro/$ (1.1389/Euro). State which currency appreciated and which depreciated, and then calculate the percentage appreciation of the currency that rose in value.

4. A trader observes that the spot rate for Japanese yen is 117.58 per U.S. dollar. The three-month forward rate for the yen is 116.91 per U.S. dollar. Calculate the forward yen premium or discount as an annual percentage rate.

5. You observe the following series of exchange rates for the U.S. dollar ($), the Canadian dollar (C $), and the Japanese yen (yen).

    $0.7237/C$ C$ 1.3818/$
    $0.0085/yen   yen 117.58/$
    C$ 0.0111/yen yen 89.81/ C$

If you have $100,00 in cash, how can you take profitable advantage of this series of exchange rates? Show the series of trades that would yield an arbitrage profit, and calculate how much profit you would make.

6. Suppose a U.S. investor can buy a risk-free 90 day Australian bond that promises a 4 percent annual nominal return. The spot exchange rate is $0.6418, which means you can exchange 0.6418, which means you can exchange 0.6418 dollar for one

Australian dollar. The 90-forward exchange rate is $0.6455. According to interest rate parity, what is the predicted risk-free interest rate in the United States?

7. Suppose that the spot exchange rate follows a random walk. An American firm owes 10 million pesos to a Mexican manufacturer. Should the firm hedge using forward contracts, and under what circumstances should the firm remain unhedged?

8. Kaman recently sold 900,000 Euros worth of electric guitars to a German distributor in Frankfurt. Delivery of the guitars and payment in Euros will occur in three months. The current spot exchange rate is $1.1256/Euro (0.8884 Euro/ $), and the 3-month forward rate is $1.1493/ Euro (0.8701 Euro/$). What risk would Kaman take if it does not hedge, and how can it hedge that risk with a forward contract? Assume that the actual exchange rate in three months is $1.1687/Euro (0.8557 Euro/ $), compute the profit or loss would Kaman have if it remains unhedged?

9. You see from the Wall street Journal that the exchange rate between the U.S. dollar and the Japanese yen is 117.58/$ ($0.0085/yen), and the exchange rate between the British pound and the U.S. dollar is 0.6114 pound /$ ($1.6355/pound). What is the exchange rate between the Japanese yen and the British pound?

10. Suppose the expected inflation in the United States equal 1 percent and expected inflation in China is 6 percent. The one-year risk-free rate in the United States is 3 percent. What would the one-year risk-free rate have to be in China to maintain real interest rate parity?

SOLUTIONS

True or False Questions

1. F	6. F
2. T	7. F
3. T	8. T
4. T	9. F
5. F	10. T

Multiple Choice Questions

1. A	6. A
2. D	7. B
3. C	8. B
4. B	9. D
5. D	10. B

Questions and Problems

1. Triangular arbitrage ensures that currency values are the same in different markets around the world. If the currency markets are not in equilibrium, than arbitrageurs will take advantage of the mispricing to make an arbitrage profit, bringing the markets back in equilibrium. Suppose the Japanese yen is overvalued relative to the British pound. A U.S. trader can earn a profit by converting U.S. dollars to the Japanese yen at the current spot rate. At the same time the trader will sell Japanese yen in Japan and buy the British pound at the pound/ yen exchange rate. Then the trader will convert the British pound into the U.S. dollars. The trader will earn a riskless arbitrage profit.

2. No, interest rate parity does not imply that interest rates are the same in all countries. Interest rate parity holds that investors should earn the same return on risk-free investments in all countries.

3. The Euro appreciated against the dollar and the dollar depreciated against the Euro. Traders exchanging Euros for dollars received more dollars per Euro in July than in May. The Euro appreciated by $(1.1389 - 1.0795)/1.0795 = 0.055$.

4. The equation to calculate the annualized forward premium or discount is:
   $$\text{Premium or discount} = \frac{\text{Forward -Spot}}{\text{Spot rate}} \times \frac{12}{n}$$

   The annualized discount of the dollar versus the yen is:
   $$\frac{116.91 - 117.58}{117.58} \times \frac{12}{3} = -0.0228 \text{ or } 2.28\% \text{ discount versus the yen.}$$

5. First, you convert U.S. dollars into Canadian dollars at the current spot rate. Starting with $100,000, this yields $1.3818 \times 100,000 = 138,180$ Canadian dollars. Then sell the Canadian dollars in Japan, receiving $89.81 \times 138,180 = 12,409,946$ yen. You convert the Japanese yen back into U.S. dollars at $117.85 \times 12,409,946 = \$105,544.70$. With this triangular arbitrage, you make a riskless profit of $105,544.70 - 100,000 = \$5,544.70$.

6. The interest rate parity equation is:
   $$\frac{0.6455}{0.6418} = \frac{(1 +(r/4))}{(1+ (0.04/4))}$$

   Solving for the 90-day interest rate in the U.S.:
   r/4 - 1.57%
   $r = (4)(1.57\%) = 6.28\%$.

7. The decision to hedge depends on what the firm expects the peso to appreciate or depreciate relative to the dollar. The American firm will buy peso forward if it expects the spot rate when the debt is due is greater than the current forward rate. By doing that, the firm will lock in the exchange rate now. If the U.S. firm expects the future spot rate to be lower than the forward rate, it will choose not to hedge.

8. Kaman has just sold 900,000 Euros. At current spot rate, this translates to a dollar sale of 900,000 x 0.8884 = $799,560. However, Kaman cannot collect the money until three months from now. The firm can hedge the sale at the 3-month forward rate, guaranteeing receipt of 900,000 x 0.8701 = $783,090. If Kaman does not hedge, and the spot rate in three months is 0.8557, the firm will have 900,000 x 0.8557 = $770,130. The firm will have a loss of $783,090 - $770,130 = $12,960 if it remains unhedged.

9. The exchange rate between the Japanese yen and the British pound is:
$$\frac{117.58 \text{ yen} / \$}{0.6114 \text{ pound}/ \$} = 192.31 \text{ yen/pound}$$

10. The real interest -rate parity equation is:

$$\frac{(1+ R \text{ China})}{(1 + 0.03)} = \frac{(1 + 0.06)}{(1 + 0.01)}$$

R China = 8.10%

21

RISK MANAGEMENT AND FINANCIAL ENGINEERING

Chapter Summary

- Increased volatility in interest rates, currency exchange rates, and commodity prices has created high demand for instruments that corporations can use to hedge these risks.

- Although it is not always in the corporation's best interest to hedge, hedging can reduce the likelihood of financial distress.

- A forward contract is an over-the-counter contract that involves two parties agreeing on a price at which the buyer will buy a fixed amount of an asset from the seller at a time in the future. A futures contract is a standardized forward contract traded on an exchange.

- The fair forward price in a forward contract is the price that eliminates any arbitrage opportunities.

- Options allow investors the ability to hedge the downside risk without giving up the upside potential. However, this comes at a cost in the form of the premium paid for the option. Swaps are long-term hedging instruments that allow corporations to change the characteristics of the periodic cash flows.

- Corporations can use financial engineering to create a specialized financial instrument to hedge a unique risk exposure.

True or False Questions

1. T   F Interest rate risk is the risk of suffering losses as a result of unanticipated changes in market rates of interest.

2. T   F Transaction exposure is the risk that a change in prices will negatively impact the value of all cash flows of a firm.

3. T   F Indirect costs of hedging include transaction costs of buying and selling forwards, future, options, and swaps.

4. T   F Closely held firms are less likely to hedge risk exposure than publicly-traded firms.

5. T   F The forward price is the price that makes the forward contract have zero net present value.

6. T   F Unless buyers or sellers of future contracts close out their positions, they are required to make or take delivery of the underlying asset.

7. T   F Short hedges involve selling a futures contract to offset an underlying short position.

8. T   F A farmer who uses orange juice futures to hedge his crop of grapefruits is tailing the hedge.

9. T   F A currency swap is the most common type of swap transaction.

10. T   F An interest rate collar is a strategy to buy an interest cap and simultaneously buy an interest rate floor.

Multiple Choice Questions

1. The risk that a change in price will negatively impact the value of all cash flows of a firm is called the:

    a. transaction exposure.
    b. economic exposure.
    c. risk management.
    d. financial engineering.

2. The forward price is the price that makes the forward contract:

    a. have zero net present value.
    b. have positive net present value.
    c. have negative net present value.
    d. undervalued.

3. The basis in a futures contract is:

    a. always positive.
    b. always negative.
    c. positive but becomes negative at maturity.
    d. equal to zero at maturity.

4. Call options on interest rates are called interest rate:

    a. floors.
    b. collars.
    c. caps.
    d. swaps.

5. Daily cash settlement of futures contracts is called:

    a. fungibility.
    b. marking-to-market.
    c. cross hedging.
    d. tailing the hedge.

6. Which of the following instruments are not traded on an exchange?

    a. futures contracts
    b. calls
    c. puts
    d. swaps

7. Which of the following instruments offer corporations the opportunity to hedge its downside risk without giving up its upside potential?

    a. options
    b. swaps
    c. futures contracts
    d. forward contracts

8. Which of the following is true of a long position in a futures contract?

    a. It gives you the right to sell an underlying asset at the futures price.
    b. It obligates you to buy at the futures price.
    c. It gives you the right to buy an underlying asset at the future price.
    d. It obligates you to sell at the futures price.

9. Hedging with a futures contract on foreign exchanges reduces currency risk; it also:
    a. maximizes the profit.
    b. eliminates the possibility of a hedge gain.
    c. provides an arbitrage opportunity.
    d. has not been popular with corporate managers.

10. Which of the following statements is false?

    a. Hedges are established to increase returns and to decrease risk from a position.

    b. Unlike forward contracts, which are customized instruments, futures are standardized.

    c. In a currency swap, two parties exchange payment obligations denominated in two different currencies.

    d. Financial engineering is the process of using the principles of financial economics to design and price financial instruments.

Questions and Problems

1. How does a futures contract differ from a forward contract?

2. What happens if a firm uses derivatives as a speculative tool rather than as a means to hedge risk?

The following data apply to the next three problems

You purchase a 5,000-bushel wheat contract at $4.10 per bushel. Your margin deposit is $4,000. The next day the wheat contract settles at $4.13 per bushel.

3. What is the balance of your margin account?

4. Three days later, the contract sells at $4.02. What is the new balance of your margin account?

5. At the end of the month, you sell the contract at $4.24 per bushel. What is the amount of gain or loss on you contract?

6. Ben Graham operates a mine in Arizona that produces gold. He anticipates having about 1,000 troy ounces of gold ready for shipment about December. Today's spot price is $392.40, and Ben is concerned that gold prices will fall between now and December 1.

    a. Suppose Ben decides to hedge his future gold production by using the December futures contract. Assume that the settlement price of $397.20 for the December contract is the relevant futures price, what type of position (long or short) should Ben take to hedge his production and what will be the gross futures price, in dollars, of his hedge? The contract size of gold futures is 100 troy ounces.

b. Now suppose that December 1 rolls around and the cash price for gold is $38850, and the December futures settlement price $390.40. If Ben decides to offset his futures contract position and deliver his 1,000 troy ounces of gold in the cash market, what is his net gain or loss on his hedge?

The following data apply to the next four problems.

Assume that you are a swap dealer and have just acted as a counterparty in an interest rate swap. The principal of the swap is $20 million, and you are obligated to make ten annual payments of 8% interest, or $1,600,000 per year. The floating rate that you will receive annually is 8.3%.

7. If interest rates do not change in the next ten years, what will your net payment be?

8. Assume a discount rate of 10%, what is the net present value of your swap?

9. If the floating rate is unchanged for four years, and then falls by 1%, what are your net payments over the ten years?

10. In the interest rate environment of problem 9, what is the NPV if the discount rate is 10%?

SOLUTIONS

True or False Questions

1. T
2. F
3. F
4. F
5. T

6. T
7. F
8. F
9. F
10. F

Multiple Choice Questions

1. B
2. A
3. D
4. C
5. B

6. D
7. A
8. B
9. B
10. A

Questions and Problems

1. Futures contracts are traded on organized exchanges, whereas forward contracts are not. Therefore, futures contracts are more liquid than forward contracts. Forward contracts specify precise delivery dates. With many futures contracts the seller can choose any delivery date during the delivery month. Futures contracts are marked to market on a daily basis. With forward contracts, cash is paid only on the delivery date.

2. If a firm uses derivatives as a speculative tool, the firm is irresponsible, and such behavior can lead to massive losses and financial disaster.

3. You gained ($4.13 - $4.10) = $0.03 per bushel, or 5,000 ($0.03) = $150. Your margin account rises to $4,150.

4. You lost (4.13 - $4.02) = $0.11 per bushel, or 5,000($0.11) = $550. Your margin account falls to $4,150 - $550 = $3,600.

5. Your gain is equal to the net price change over the life of your trade:
       ($4.24 - $4.10)(5,000) = $700.

6. a. Ben should short 10 December futures contracts (10 x 100 oz = 1,000 oz) to protect his gold production in the event of a decline in the price of gold. The gross futures price of his hedge is (1,000)($397.20) = $397,200.

   b. Ben will buy back his ten December futures contracts. His loss in the cash market is ($392.40 - $388.50)(1,000) = -$3,900. His gain in the futures market is ($397.20 - $390.40)(1,000) = $6,800. His net gain is $2,900.

7. You will pay $1.6 million and receive $1.66 million floating, for a net inflow of $60,000 per year.

8. You have an annuity of ten years with a payment of $60,000, discounted at 10%. The present value of the annuity is:
   PV = ($60,000)(6.1446) = $368,676.

9. For the first four years, you will pay $1.6 million and receive $1.66 million, for a net inflow of $60,000 per year. In the remaining six years, you continue to pay $1.6 million, but your new inflow will be $1.46 million. Therefore, you have a net outflow of $140,000 per year from year 5 to year 10.

10. The NPV of your swap is:
    NPV = $60,000 (PVIFA at 10%,4) - ($140,000)(PVIFA 10%,6)(PVIF at 10%,4)
    = $60,000(3.1699) - $140,000(4.3553)(0.683)
    = $190,194 - $416,454 = -$226,260

22
STRATEGIC AND OPERATIONAL FINANCIAL PLANNING

Chapter Summary

- Strategic (long-term) financial plans act as guides for preparing operating (short-term) financial plans. Finance acts as a business partner with other functional units in developing the firm's strategic plan.

- The sustainable growth model is a model that managers can use to determine the feasibility of a target growth rate under certain conditions. When the growth rate that maximizes shareholder value does not match the sustainable rate, the firm must adjust to achieve the desired growth rate.

- Pro-forma financial statements are projected financial statements, typically based on the historical financial relations within the firm. Pro-forma income statements can be prepared by using the percentage-of-sales method, or by breaking all costs and expenses into fixed and variable components.

- Cash budgets forecast the short-term cash inflow and outflows of a firm. Financial managers often applies sensitivity analysis to cash budgets to assess financial needs under the most adverse situations.

True or False Questions

1. T   F A major contribution of finance to the strategic planning process involves risk management.

2. T   F The sustainable growth model shows how rapidly a firm can grow while maintaining a balance between its sources and uses of funds.

3. T   F If a firm increases its dividend payout ratio, the sustainable growth rate will rise.

4. T   F The top-down sales forecast begins by talking with customers to assess the demand.

5. T   F Firms that follow the matching strategy finance permanent assets with long-term funding sources, and they finance their seasonal asset requirements with short-term debt.

6. T   F The primary tool for managing cash flow on a long-term basis is the cash budget.

7. T   F A cash budget is a statement of the firm's planned inflows and outflows of cash.

8. T   F The most common cash disbursements are cash purchases, fixed asset outlays, and depreciation expense.

9. T   F A cash budget forecasts long-term cash inflows and outflows.

10. T   F Any action that accelerates payments to suppliers will increase monthly cash surplus.

Multiple Choice Questions

1. An increase in which of the following variables will make the sustainable growth rate decline?

    a. profit margin.
    b. dividend payout ratio
    c. total asset turnover ratio
    d. asset-to-equity ratio

2. Which of the following is not an assumption of the sustainable growth model?

    a. The firm's net profit margin is constant.
    b. The firm will issue no new shares of common stock next year.
    c. The firm pays out a constant dollar amount of dividends.
    d. The firm maintains a constant asset-to-equity ratio.

3. Which of the following financing strategies does a firm employ if it uses short-term borrowing to finance the seasonal peaks each year as well as a portion of the long-term growth in sales and assets?

    a. a conservative strategy
    b. an aggressive strategy
    c. a matching strategy
    d. a neutral strategy

4. The key input required in forecasting a firm's future development is its:

    a. profit.
    b. sales.
    c. cash flow.
    d. assets.

5. Which of the following items does not fluctuate with sales?

    a. inventory
    b. accounts payable
    c. cost of goods sold
    d. level of debt

6. Which of the following items on the balance sheet is most likely to be affected by a change in sales:

    a. cash
    b. notes payable
    c. common stock
    d. paid-in capital

7. Which of the following income statement items is least likely to be affected by a drastic change in sales from year to year?

    a. cost of goods sold
    b. earnings per share
    c. preferred stock dividends
    d. net operating income

8. The key to creating an accurate pro-forma income statement is a good:

    a. pro-forma balance sheet.
    b. forecast of profit.
    c. sales forecast.
    d. pro-forma sources and uses of funds statement.

9. Which of the following balance sheet accounts is least likely to be affected by a large change in sales?

    a. inventory
    b. cash
    c. accounts payable
    d. preferred stock

10. Which of the following statements is false?

    a. The key inputs to pro-forma statements are financial statements from the preceding year, the sales forecast for the coming year, and a variety of assumptions

    b. An increase in the ratio of assets-to-equity will reduce the sustainable growth rate.

    c. A major contribution of finance to the strategic planning process involves risk management.

    d. Top-down sales forecasts rely heavily on macroeconomic and industry forecasts.

Questions and Problems

1. Explain the percentage-of-sales method for calculating pro-forma statements.

2. Describe the top-down and bottom-up sales forecasting methods.

3. EMC reported the following data in its most recent annual report:

Sales	$99 million
Net income	$5.8 million
Dividends	$1.2 million
Assets	$71 million

    EMC is financed with 80 percent equity. What is EMC's sustainable growth rate?

4. Certain liabilities and stockholders' equity items generally increase spontaneously with increases in sales. Identify those items that typically increase spontaneously.

    Accounts receivable
    Notes payable
    Accounts payable
    Inventory
    Debentures
    Common Stock

5. Suppose a firm makes the following changes. If the change means that the sustainable growth rate will increase, indicate this by a (+); indicate a decrease by a (-); and indicate indeterminate or no effect by a (0).

   a. The dividend payout ratio is increased.   _____
   b. The firm's profit margin declines due to increased competition.   _____
   c. The firm's debt-to-equity ratio rises from 0.1 to 0.2.   _____
   d. The firm substitutes long-term debentures for short-term bank loans.   _____
   e. The firm increases its total asset turnover ratio by improving efficiency. _____

6. Toro makes 30% of its sales for cash, 20% on 30 days credit, and 50% on 60 days credit.

   a. What is the average credit period Toro extends to its customers?
   b. Toro's daily sales amount to $5 million. The cost of goods sold is 70% of sales. How much cash does Toro need to finance accounts receivable?

The following data apply to the next four problems.

In 2002, Dial Corp. forecasts that its sales will increase by 10% each year for the next three years, and that fixed costs will increase by 25% in 2003, 15% in 2004, and then remains unchanged in 2005. The liabilities, which increase automatically with sales, will increase 20% a year for the next three years and its net income and dividends will increase by 10% a year. Additional data for 2002:

Fixed assets	$400,000
Sales	1,600,000
Account payable	90,000
Net Income	50,000
Dividends	10,000

7. What are the external funds required (EFR) for Dial in 2003?

8. What are the external funds required for Dial in 2004 and 2005?

9. If Dial changes its payout ratio to 50% in 2003, what would be the EFR?

10. If Dial decides to distribute all of its net income as dividends in 2004, what would be its EFR?

SOLUTIONS

True or False Questions

1. T	6. F
2. T	7. T
3. F	8. F
4. F	9. F
5. T	10. F

Multiple Choice Questions

1. B	6. A
2. C	7. C
3. B	8. C
4. B	9. D
5. D	10. B

Questions and Problems

1. The percentage-of-sales method assumes that most accounts increase or decrease proportionally with sales. Although the relation is not completely linear, the percentage-of-sales method provides a rough guideline to estimate external funds required.

2. A top-down sales forecast relies on macroeconomic and industry forecasts. A firm could use a statistical model or subscribe to forecasts produced by firms specializing in econometric modeling. Senior managers establish a firm -wide objective for increased sales. Then division heads pass down sales targets to people below. The bottom-up method for forecasting sales begins by talking with customers. Estimates from each division are added and passed up to senior managers to create an overall forecast for the company.

3. EMC's sustainable growth rate depends on its profit margin, dividend payout ratio, assets to equity, and assets to sales ratios.
   EMC's profit margin is net income/sales = 5.8/99 = 0.0586.
   Dividend payout = dividends/ net income = 1.2/5.8 = 0.2069.
   Assets to equity = assets/equity = 100%/80% = 1.25.
   Assets to sales = 71/99 = 0.7122.

The sustainable growth rate of EMC is:

$$g = \frac{m(1-d) \, A/E}{(A/S) - [m(1-d) \, A/E]}$$

$$= \frac{0.0586 \, (1 - 0.2069)1.25}{0.7172 - [0.0586(1-0.2069)0.7172]}$$

$$- \, 0.0581/(0.7172\text{-}0.0333) = 8.49\%.$$

4. Items that typically increase spontaneously with increases in sales are: accounts receivable, notes payable, accounts payable, and inventory.

5.   a. -
       b. -
       c. +
       d. 0
       e. +

6. a. The average credit Toro extends to its customers is:

    (0.3)(0 days) +(0.2)(30 days) + (0.5)(60 days) = 36 days.

  b. The cost of goods sold per day is 0.7 x $5 million = $3.5 million.
    The investment required in accounts receivable:
    ($3.5 million)(36 days) = $126 million.

7. The external funds required for Dial in 2003 are:

        EFR = Required increase in assets - Increase in automatic liability - (Next year's income - Dividend)
        = ($400,000)(0.25) - ($90,000)(0.2) - [$50,000(1.1) - $10,000(1.1)]
        = 100,000 - 18,000 - (55,000 -11,000) = $38,000.

8. The external funds required for Dial in 2004 are:

    EFR = (500,000)(0.15) - (180,000)(0.2) - [50,000(1.1) - 11,000(1.1)]
       = 75,00 - 21,600 - (60,500 - 12,100) = $5,000.

    Because Dial's fixed costs are unchanged in 2005, the required increase in assets and the EFR will be zero.

9. The new EFR in 2003 is:

    EFR = 100,000 - 18,000 - [55,000 -(0,5)(55,000)] = $54,500.

10. If Dial distributes all of its net income as dividends in 2004, its EFR is:

    EFR = 75,000 - 21,600 - (60,500 - 60,500) = $53,400.

23

SHORT-TERM FINANCIAL MANAGEMENT

Chapter Summary

- The cash conversion cycle has three main components: the average age of inventory (AAI), the average collection period (ACP), and the average payment period (APP). The operating cycle (OC) is the sum of AAI and ACP. The cash conversion cycle is OC - APP.

- The financial manager's focus in managing the firms' short-term activities is to shorten the cash conversion cycle. The basic strategies are to turn inventory quickly, collect accounts receivable quickly, pay accounts slowly, and manage mail, processing, and clearing time.

- The objective for managing accounts receivables is to collect accounts as quickly as possible without losing sales. The key aspects of accounts receivable management include credit standards, credit terms, collection policy, and credit monitoring. Cash discounts can be used to encourage customers to pay early.

- Two popular approaches to credit selection are the use of five Cs of credit and credit scoring.

- The cash manager's role is to manage the cash flow timeline related to collection, concentration, and disbursement of the company's funds. The cash manager is also responsible for financial relationships, cash flow forecasting, investing, borrowing, and information management. In managing collections, the cash manager can reduce collection float using various collection measures, such as field-banking systems, mail-based systems, and electronic systems.

- The objective for managing the firm's accounts payable is to pay accounts slowly without damaging the firm's credit rating. Financial managers can use popular disbursement methods such as zero-balance accounts, controlled disbursement, and positive pay.

- Cash managers can hold near-cash assets in the form of short-term investments to earn a return on temporary excess cash balances. Short-term borrowing can be obtained by issuing commercial paper and through lines of credit.

True or False Questions

1. T   F   Operating assets include cash, marketable securities, accounts receivable, and inventories that are necessary for the day-to-day operation of the firm.

2. T   F The cash conversion cycle has two main components: average collection period and average payment period.

3. T   F The average collection period is the average length of time from a sale on credit until the payment becomes usable funds for the firm.

4. T   F Credit scoring provides a framework for performing in-depth credit analysis but it does not provide a specific accept or reject decision.

5. T   F In general, tightening credit standards will yield the benefit of increased unit sales, but it will also yield higher costs from additional investment in accounts receivable.

6. T   F Terms of 2/10 net 60 mean the customer has 60 days from the beginning of the credit period to pay the full invoice amount.

7. T   F The aging of accounts receivable is the normal timing in which a firm's customers pay their accounts, expressed as the percentage of monthly sales collected in each month following the sale.

8. T   F Float refers to funds that have been sent by the payer but are not yet usable funds to the payee.

9. T   F Speeding up collections reduces customer collection float time and thus reduces the firm's average collection period.

10. T   F Zero-balance accounts are disbursement accounts that have an end-of-day balance of zero most of the time.

Multiple Choice Questions

1. The cash conversion cycle is equal to the operating cycle less:

    a. the average payment period on accounts payable.
    b. the average collection period.
    c. the average age of inventory.
    d. the average holding period of marketable securities.

2. To shorten the cash conversion cycle, a firm can:

    a. collect accounts receivable as quickly as possible.
    b. pay accounts as quickly as possible.
    c. turn over inventory as slowly as possible.
    d. reduce processing and clearing time when paying vendors.

3. The cash conversion cycle is equal to:

    a. the operating cycle + average payment period.
    b. the average age of inventory + average collection period + average payment period.
    c. the average age of inventory + average collection period - average payment period.
    d. the operating cycle - average collection period - average payment period.

4. The operating cycle ends with collection of cash from the sale of the finished product. At what point does the operating cycle begin?

    a. arrival of merchandise
    b. ordering merchandise
    c. payment for merchandise
    d. sale of merchandise

5. Which of the following is not a source of short-term financing?

    a. line of credit
    b. bonds
    c. commercial paper
    d. accounts payable

6. Which of the following is not one of the five C's of credit?

    a. capital
    b. credit scoring
    c. collateral
    d. character

7. The term 2/10 net 30 means:

    a. The customer can take a 2 percent discount from the invoice amount if payment is made immediately, or the customer can pay the full amount within 30 days
    b. The customer has 30 days from the beginning of the credit period to pay the full invoice amount.
    c. The customer can take a 2 percent discount from the invoice amount if payment is made within 10 days, or the customer can pay the full amount within 30 days.
    d. The customer can take a 2 percent discount from the invoice amount if payment is made within 30 days.

8. Zero-balance accounts are:

   a. disbursement accounts that always **have** an end-of-day balance of zero.
   b. accounts that receive early notification of checks that will be presented against such accounts on a given day.
   c. checking account that has an end-of-day balance of zero most of the time.
   d. sweep accounts in which the bank sweeps account surpluses into an interest-earning account.

9. The time between deposit of the check and presentation of the check back to the bank on which it is drawn is called the:

   a. availability float.
   b. processing float.
   c. mail float.
   d. clearing float.

10. Which of the following statements is false?

    a. Credit scoring is most commonly used by large credit card operations.
    b. Only large firms benefit from a lockbox system because their customers are geographically dispersed.
    c. Cash concentration is the process of bringing the lockbox and other deposits together into one bank, called the concentration bank.
    d. The prime rate is the rate of interest changed by largest U.S. bank on short-term loans to business borrowers with good credit ratings.

Questions and Problems.

1. Describe three ways a firm can reduce its net working capital.

2. State various current liabilities a firm can use as sources of short-term financing to cover a temporary cash deficit.

3. Global Crossing buys $3.5 million of inventory every day for a month from a supplier that offers the firms credit 2/10 net 40. Global Crossing is in financial distress, so it delays payment until the end of the 40 days. What is the total amount of short-term financing from accounts payable?

4. Joslyn's current assets are $95 million, and its total assets are $380 million. Long-term liabilities and stockholders' equity total $305 million.

   a. What are Joslyn's current liabilities?
   b. What is Joslyn's net working capital?

5. Dell Computers is trying to improve its management of operating assets and liabilities. Inventories have an average of 80 days, and accounts receivable have an average of 45 days. Accounts payable are paid approximately 40 days after they arrive. Dell has annual sales of $96 million, its cost of goods sold represents 70 percent of sales, and its purchases represent 75 percent of cost of goods sold. Assume a 365-day year.

    a. Calculate the firm's operating cycle
    b. Calculate the firms' cash conversion cycle (CCC)
    c. Calculate the amount of total resources Dell has invested in its CCC.

6. Sears is considering four plans that affect several current accounts. Given the four plans and their effects on inventory, receivables, and payables, as shown in the following table, which plan should Sears select? Explain.

	Change		
	Avg. age inventory	Avg. collection period	Avg. payment period
Plan	(days) (days)	(days)	
A	+20	+15	-5
B	+15	-25	+10
C	-10	-5	0
D	-20	+5	+10

7. Hallmark is considering installing a just-in-time inventory system in order to reduce its in-process inventories. The annual cost of the system is $195,000. Hallmark estimates that with this system, the average inventory investment will decline by 30 percent from its current level of $3.95 million. All other costs are unaffected by this system. Hallmark can earn 16 percent per year on equal-risk investments.

    a. What is the annual cost savings expected to result from installing the just-in-time inventory system?
    b. Should Hallmark install the system? Explain.

8. Nautilus Company currently has an average collection period of 50 days and annual sales of $910 million. Assume a 365-day year.

    a. What is the firm's average accounts receivable balance?
    b. If the variable cost of each product is 70 percent of sales, what is the average investment in accounts receivable?
    c. If the equal-risk opportunity cost of the investment in accounts receivable is 10 percent, what is the total annual cost of the resources invested in accounts receivable?

9. Indicate by (+), (-), or (0) whether each of the following events would probably cause accounts receivable (A/R), sales, and profits to increase, decrease, or be affected in an indeterminate manner:

	A/R	Sales	Profits
a) The firm relaxes its credit standards	___	___	___
b) The firm changes its cash discount from 2/10, net 30 to 2/10 net 40	___	___	___
c) The firm raises the credit score from 65 to 75. Now only applications with a score of 75 or above will be accepted.	___	___	___

10. Determine the interest rate associated with not taking the cash discount and paying at the end of the credit period for the following cash discount terms. Assume a 365-day year

    a. 2/10 net 40
    b. 1/10 net 60
    c. 2/10 net 60

SOLUTIONS

True or False Questions

1. T		6. F
2. F		7. F
3. T		8. T
4. F		9. T
5. F		10. F

Multiple Choice Questions

1. A		6. B
2. A		7. C
3. C		8. A
4. A		9. D
5. B		10. B

Questions and Problems

1. A firm can reduce its net working capital by reducing the average collection period, or extending the average payment period.

2. A firm can use accounts payable, short-term bank loans, a line of credit, or a revolving agreement as sources of short-term financing to cover a temporary cash deficit.

3. Global Crossing's total amount of short-term financing from account payable is:
   ($3.5 million)(40 days) = $140 million

4. a. Joslyn's current liabilities are:
      Current liabilities = Total Assets - Long-term liabilities and equity
                          = $380 million - $305 million
                          = $75 million.

   b. Joslyn's net working capital is:
      $95 million - $75 million = $20 million.

5. a. The firm's operating cycle is the sum of its average age of the inventory and average collection period = 80 days + 45 days = 125 days.

   b. CCC = OC - APP = 125 - 40 = 85 days.

   c. Resources invested in the cash conversion cycle are:
      Inventory = $96,000,000 x 70% 80/365 = $14,728,767
         + Accounts receivable = $96,000,000 x 45/365 = $11,835,617
         - Accounts payable = $96,000,000 x 70% x 75% 40/365 = $5,523,288
         = Resources invested of $21,041,096.

6.

Plan	Avg. age of inventory (days)	Avg. collection period (days)	Avg. payment period (days)	Change in CCC (I+C-P)
A	+20	+15	-5	+40
B	+15	-25	+10	-20
C	-10	-5	0	-15
D	-20	+5	+10	-25

   Sears should select plan D because it results in the biggest reduction (25 days) in the cash conversion cycle.

7. a. The inventory investment will decline by $3.95 million x 30% = $1,185,000. This decline will save Hallmark $1,185,000 per year.

   b. The net present value of the just-in-time inventory system is:

   NPV = 189,600 - 195,000 = -5,400

   Hallmark should not install the system because its NPV is negative.

8. a. Nautilus' average receivable balance is $910,000,000 x 50/365 = $124,657,534.

   b. The total variable cost is:

   $910,000,000 x 70% x 50/365 = $87,260,274.

   c. The total annual cost of resources invested in accounts receivable is:

   $87,260,274 x 10% = $8,726,027.

9.

	A/R	Sales	Profits
a.	+	+	0
b.	+	0	0
c.	-	-	0

10. r = d/(1-d) x 365/(CP-DP)

   a. 2/10 net 40

   .02/(1-.02) x 365/(40-10) = 24.83%.

   b. 1/10 net 60

   .01/(1-.01) x 365/(60-10) = 7.37%.

   c. 2/10 net 60

   .02/(1-.02) x 365/(60-10) = 14.90%.

24

MERGERS, ACQUISITIONS, AND CORPORATE CONTROL

Chapter Summary

- Mergers and acquisitions are major corporate finance events that can help managers achieve the goal of maximizing shareholder wealth. Managers have either value-maximizing or non-value maximizing motives for pursuing mergers. Value-maximizing motive include expansion into new markets, capturing size economies or other synergies, establishing market power, or generating free cash flow to make better investments. Agency problems result in such non-value-maximizing motives as empire building, entrenchment, hubris, and diversification.

- Corporate control activities are regulated by federal, state, and international authorities. Federal antitrust legislation has been developed for over a century. The William Act established disclosure requirements for ownership in public corporations, and regulation of tender offers. Federal security laws also prohibit corporate insiders from trading on the nonpublic information of a pending takeover.

- Empirical research finds the following results: target shareholders almost always win, white knights almost always lose, and other acquirers' returns are mixed. The combined value of merging firms also increases, especially in nonconglomerate combinations. Long-term performance is highest for focus-increased deals financed with cash and lowest for diversifying mergers financed with stock.

True or False Questions

1. T   F   Under statutory merger, both the acquirer and target disappear as separate corporations and combine to form an entirely new corporation with new common stock.

2. T   F   A two-tiered offer results when the acquirer offers to buy a certain number of shares at one price and then more shares at another price.

3. T   F   In a split-off, a parent company sells all of its subsidiaries so that it ceases to exist.

4. T   F   Vertical mergers are combinations of companies with similar but not exact lines of business.

5. T   F   Economies of scale occur when a merger results in less-volatile cash flows, lowering default risk, and a lower cost of capital.

6. T   F   Empirical results indicate that the diversification motive is now viewed as a value-destroying rationale caused by agency problems.

7. T   F   Antitrust legislation is intended to prevent an anticompetitive business environment.

8. T   F   A Herfindahl-Hirschman Index of 1800 or higher indicates that the industry is moderately concentrated.

9. T   F   Acquiring-firm stockholders almost always experience substantial wealth gain in successful mergers.

10. T   F   Empirical evidence strongly supports the notion that mergers that decrease focus cause a loss in firm value.

Multiple Choice Questions

1. A transaction in which the acquirer has a lesser market value than the target is called a:

    a. consolidation.
    b. reverse merger.
    c. leveraged-buyout.
    d. subsidiary merger.

2. The percent of any corporations's stock that an individual can own before facing the requirement of filing with the Securities and Exchange Commission is:

    a. 3 percent.
    b. 5 percent.
    c. 7 percent.
    d. 10 percent.

3. Which of the following transactions does not generate any cash inflow into the parent company?

    a. equity carve-outs
    b. split-ups
    c. spin-offs
    d. divestitures

4. Combinations of companies with similar but not exact lines of business are called:

    a. product extension mergers
    b. vertical mergers
    c. horizontal mergers
    d. market extension mergers

5. Operating synergies are least likely to be realized in:

   a. horizontal mergers.
   b. vertical mergers.
   c. market extension mergers.
   d. conglomerate mergers.

6. Which of the following theories claims that poorly monitored mangers will pursue mergers to maximize their corporation's asset size?

   a. the hubris hypothesis of corporate takeovers
   b. the managerialism theory of mergers
   c. the free cash flow theory of mergers
   d. the managerial entrenchment theory of mergers

7. Which of the following numbers Herfindahl-Hirschman Index indicates that an industry or market is highly concentrated?

   a. 1,000
   b. 1,400
   c. 1,700
   d. 1,900

8. Which of the following groups almost always loses in a merger?

   a. target shareholders
   b. shareholders of acquiring firms
   c. shareholders of white knight acquirers
   d. shareholders of target's competing firms

9. The discount that diversified firms trade relative to their focused counterparts is about:

   a. 5 percent
   b. 10 percent
   c. 15 percent
   d. 20 percent

10. The percentage of unrelated acquisitions that are eventually divested is about:

    a. 50 percent.
    b. 60 percent.
    c. 30 percent.
    d. 15 percent.

Questions and Problems

1. Explain how an acquirer can use a hostile tender offer to take over another firm.

2. Explain the Herfindahl-Hirschman Index (HHI). How is this index used to measure a range of concentration levels in an industry?

3. GM is offering as consideration for merger target Dana 0.5 share of its stock for each shareof Dana. There are 10 million shares of Dana outstanding, and its stock price was $15 before the merger offer. GM's pre-offer stock price was $40. What is the control premium percentage offered?

4. Harrah Corporation is planning an acquisition. Harrah's market value is $25 million and Harrah has $10 million in debt. Harrah can acquire Park Place, with a market value is $8 million and no debt. Alternatively, Harrah can acquire MGM, which has $6 million in debt. MGM has 1 million shares outstanding, trading at $16 per share. If Harrah buys Park Place, the market value of the combined company will be $30 million. If Harrah buys MGM, the value of the combined company will be $40 million. Assume that the weighted average cost of capital will not be affected. Which company should Harrah acquire?

5. Janus is planning to make a tender offer for CSX. Janus' weighted average cost of capital is15%, CSX's is 13%, and the combined company's will be 14%. Janus has $20 million of debt and CSX has $10 million. Janus expects a perpetual cash flow of $4 million, and CSX expects cash flows of $1,600,000. The combined company will have a cash flow of $5.9 million. Debt will not be issued or retired after the acquisition. Should Janus acquire CSX? Explain.

6. Kimberly Clark plans to acquire Vu Company. Kimberly Clark has an equity value of $510 million. Vu's equity value is $60 million. Each firm has 10 million shares outstanding. The combined firm is expected to have a value of $590 million. If Kimberly Clark offers $10 cash for each share of Vu, find the cost of the transaction. Should Kimberly Clark acquire Vu?

7. ITT is considering the acquisition of Big Joe Industries. Managers at ITT estimated the incremental benefit of the acquisition to be $3.1 million. The current market value of Big Joe's equity is $9 million, and the firm has 600,000 shares outstanding. What is the maximum price ITT should pay?

8. ITW estimates that the acquisition of Signode will provide a synergistic benefit of $4 million. The market price of Signode is $25 million. Based on the following cash payments to acquire Signode, how much of the benefit will go to ITW shareholders and how much will go to Signode shareholders? Possible payments are $25 million, $27 million, $29 million, and $30 million.

9. Zayre is offering an exchange of shares in an attempt to take over K-mart. Zayre has 200,000 shares of stock outstanding valued at $5 a share. K-Mart has 100,00 shares outstanding at $3 a share. The combined firm will have a value of $2 million. K-Mart managers believe that its stock is undervalued and demand a 30% premium over market value to accept the offer. How many shares must Zayre offer for each outstanding share of K-Mart in order for K-Mart to accept its offer?

10. Refer back to problem 9. If Zayre refuses to pay any premium over the market value of K-Mart, how many shares should Zayre offer for each share of K-Mart?

SOLUTIONS
True or False Questions
1.	F	6.	T
2.	T	7.	T
3.	F	8.	F
4.	F	9.	F
5.	F	10.	T

Multiple Choice Questions
1.	B	6.	B
2.	B	7.	D
3.	C	8.	C
4.	A	9.	C
5.	D	10.	A

Questions and Problems

1. In a hostile tender offer, an acquirer asks the target shareholders to tender their shares without the consent of the target's management. If the acquirer can buy more than 50% of the targets shares, the acquirer has complete control.

2. The HHI is calculated as the sum of the squares of each company's percentage of sales within an industry. If the HHI>1800, the industry is highly concentrated. If the HHI is between 1000 to 1800, the industry is moderately concentrated. If the HHI is below 1,000, the industry is not concentrated.

3. The pre-offer value of Dana is $150 million (10 million shares x $15 share), and GM offered 0.5 Share of its own stock (worth $40/share) as payment, or $20 per share of Dana stock. The initial control premium offered is $5/share ($20 offer price - $15 market price of Dana stock). The control premium percentage is $5/$15 = 33%.

4. The value of Harrah's equity is:
   $25 million - $10 million = $15 million.
   Park Place has no debt, so the value of its equity is $8 million. The incremental
   benefit from buying Park Place is:
   $30 million - $15 million - $8 million = $7 million.

   MGM's equity is:
   ($16)(1 million shares) = $16 million.

   The incremental profit from buying MGM is:
   $40 million - $15 million - $16 million = $9 million.

   Both potential acquisitions have positive incremental benefit. If Harrah has no capital
   constraint, it should buy both firms. If Harrah can only buy one firm, Harrah should
   buy MGM because the incremental benefit is higher.

5. The market value of Janus is:
   $4,000,000/0.15 = $26,666,667.

   The equity value of Janus is:
   $26,666,667 - $20,000,000 = $6,666,667.

   The market value of CSX is:
   $1,600,000/0.13 = $12,307692.

   The equity value of CSX is:
   $12,307,692 - $10,000,000 = $2,307,692.

   The combined market value of two firms is:
   $5,900,000/0.14 = $42,142,857.

   The combined equity value of two firms is:
   $42,142,857 - $30,000,000 = $12,142,857.

   The incremental benefit is:
   $12,142,857 - $6,666,667 - $2,307,692 = $3,168,498.
   Janus should acquire CSX because the incremental benefit is positive.

6. The cost to Kimberly Clark is the price paid for Vu's equity:
   Cost = $10 x 10,000,000 = $100,000,000.
   The NPV of the acquisition is;
   $590,000,000 - $510,000,000 -$100,000,000 = -$20 million.

   The NPV is negative, so Kimberly Clark should not proceed with the acquisition.

7. The value of each share of Big Joe is:
   $9,000,000/600,000 = $15.

   The maximum premium that ITT can offer is:
   $3,100,000/$9,000,000 = 34.44%.

   The maximum price ITT should offer is:
   $15 x 1.3444 =$20.17 per share or $12,099,600.

8. If ITW pays only $25 million, the entire $4 million benefit will accrue to ITW
   shareholders. At other prices:

Payment	ITW holder Gain (loss)	Signode holder Gain (loss)	Total Benefit
$25	$4	$0	$4
27	2	2	4
29	0	4	4
30	(1)	5	4

9. K-Mart's current market value is:
   $3 x 100,000 = $300,000.

   K-Mart managers want the total offer price to be:
   $300,000 x 1.3 = $390,000.

   The payment represents $390,000/$2,000,000 = 19.5% of the combined firm's
   stock. Therefore, Zayre must give 19.5% of the post-acquisition number of shares
   outstanding:

   n/(200,000 + n) = 19.5%
   n = 48,477 shares.

   Zayre must issue 48,477 shares to take over K-Mart. Because K-Mart has
   100,000 shares outstanding, Zayre must exchange approximately one share of its
   stock for every two shares of K-Mart (100,000/48,447 = 2.06 share).

10. If Zayre pays no premium, the offer price will be $300,000 or ($300,000/$2,000,000)
    = 15 percent of the combined firm's stock. The number of shares to issue will be:

    n/(200,000 + n) = 0.15
    n = 35,294 shares.

    Zayre will offer one share for every (100,000/35,294) = 2.83 shares of K-Mart.

25
BANKRUPTCY AND FINANCIAL DISTRESS

Chapter Summary

- A business can fail in two ways. When it cannot pay its liabilities when they come due, the firm is technically insolvent due to a liquidity crisis. When its liabilities exceed the fair market value of its assets, the firm is insolvent. Bankruptcy occurs when a company comes under the authority of a bankruptcy court, which exercises control over the firm.

- Mismanagement is the primary cause of business failure. Other causes are economic downturns and corporate maturity.

- Companies facing financial distress can voluntarily reorganize or liquidate. By acting voluntarily, firms reduce the legal and administrative express associated with a formal bankruptcy filing.

- Firms can reorganize with Chapter 11 by means of the unanimous consent procedure or the **cramdown** procedure. In a reorganization, the terms of the debt can be relaxed by extending the payment term or lowering the interest rate.

- Firms are liquidated under Chapter 7 by means of the absolute priority rule, which ranks creditors in terms of the order of their claims for payment from the proceeds of the liquidation of the firm's assets.

- The likelihood of bankruptcy can be predicted with a fair degree of accuracy using Altman's Z score.

True or False Questions

1. T   F   Insolvency bankruptcy occurs when a firm is unable to pay its liabilities as claims come due.

2. T   F   The primary cause of business failure is economic downturns.

3. T   F   An extension is an arrangement wherein the firm's creditors are promised payment in full, although not immediately.

4. T   F   Chapter 11 of the Bankruptcy Reform Act describes the procedures to be followed when liquidating a failed firm.

5. T   F   Upon filing of a reorganization petition, the filing firm becomes the debtor in possession of the assets, and the bankrupt firm's existing management is usually replaced.

6. T   F   Under recapitalization of a firm's capital structure, debts are generally exchanged for equity or the maturities of existing debts are extended.

7. T   F   Under unanimous consent procedure, all members of equity classes and creditors must consent unanimously to the reorganization plan.

8. T   F   When firms file for bankruptcy, their obligation to pay interest to pre-bankruptcy creditors, both secured and unsecured, ceases.

9. T   F   The Altman's Z score has been found to be about 90 percent accurate in forecasting bankruptcy one year in the future.

10. T   F   Firms that reorganize lose their accrued tax loss carryforwards.

Multiple Choice Questions

1.   When a firm's liabilities exceed the fair market value of its assets, the firm is :

a. technically insolvent.
b. bankrupt.
c. insolvent.
d. liquidated.

2.   The largest bankruptcy in U.S. history as of 2001 is:

a. Texaco, Inc.
b. Enron Corp.
c. Pacific Gas and Electric Co.
d. Financial Corp. of America.

3.   A pre rata cash settlement of creditor claims is called a(n):

a. composition.
b. creditor control.
c. assignment.
d. extension.

4.   Which of the following Chapters in the Bankruptcy Reform Act of 1978 outlines the procedures for reorganizing a failed firm?

a. chapter 1
b. chapter 7
c. chapter 9
d. chapter 11

5.   Which of the following is not required under reorganization plans using the unanimous consent procedure (UCP) ?

a. A company must be solvent to use the UCP.
b. Creditors and equity classes must consent unanimously to the reorganization plan.
c. Each class of unsecured creditors must vote for the reorganization plan by an 80% margin.
d. Each secured creditor is a class, and each must vote for the plan if its claims are impaired.

6.   Which of the following claims has the highest priority according to the absolute priority rules?

a. the expenses of administering the bankruptcy proceedings
b. claims of secured creditors
c. taxes owed to the federal government
d. wages that have been earned by workers

7.   Which of the following groups has the lowest priority according to the absolute priority rules?

a. Preferred stockholders
b. Common stockholders
c. Unsecured creditors
d. Debenture holders

8.   Which of the following Altman's Z score has the highest probability of failure?

a. 1.6
b. 1.8
c. 2.7
d. 3.1

9.   The Altman's Z score has been found to be about _____ percent accurate in forecasting bankruptcy two years in the future

    a. 60
    b. 70
    c. 80
    d. 90

10.   Which of the following statements is true?

    a. Firms in reorganization can reject their collective bargaining labor agreements.
    b. Firms in reorganization can reject any of their contracts.
    c. Firms that liquidate retain most of their accrued tax loss carryforwards.
    d. When firms file for bankruptcy, they must continue to pay interest to prebankruptcy creditors.

Questions and Problems

1. Why do creditors usually accept a plan for voluntary reorganization rather than demand liquidation of a business?

2. Explain why the Altman's Z score is useful to a firm as well as its investors.

3. Enron can be liquidated for $9 million, or it can be reorganized. Reorganization would require an investment of $4 million. If Enron is reorganized, earnings are projected to be $900,000 per year, and the company would trade at a price/earnings ratio of 15 times. Should Enron be liquidated or reorganized?

4. UAL has outstanding debt of $650 million. Classify each of the following voluntary settlements as an extension, a composition, or a combination of the two

    a. Paying a group of creditors 70 cents on the dollar immediately and paying the remaining creditors 60 cents on the dollar in four periodic installments.
    b. Paying all creditors in full in 500 days.
    c. Paying a group of creditors with claim of $150 million in full over three years and immediately paying the remaining creditors 65 cents on the dollar.

The following data apply to the next four problems.

Apollo Industries recently ran into financial difficulties that have resulted in the initiation of voluntary settlement procedures. The firm currently has $20 million in outstanding debt and approximately $9 million in marketable short-term assets. Indicate, for each of the following plans, whether the plan in an extension, composition, or a combination of the two. Also indicate the cash payments and timing of the payments required of the firm under each plan.

5. Each creditor will be paid 45 cents on the dollar immediately, and the debts will be considered fully satisfied.

6. Each creditor will be paid in full amount of its claims in three installments of 40 cents, 30 cents, and 30 cents on the dollar. The installments will be made in 90 -day intervals, beginning in 90 days.

7. A group of creditors with claim of $4 million will be paid immediately in full; the rest will be paid 40 cents on the dollar, payable in 90 days.

8. Each creditor will be paid 50 cents on the dollar in two quarterly installments of 30 cents and 20 cents. The first installment is to be paid in 60 days.

9. Sysco has a working capital/ total assets ratio of 0.3, a retained earnings/ total assets ratio of 0.15, an earnings before interest and taxes/ total assets ratio of 0.1, a market value of equity/ book value of debt ratio of 0.4, and sales/total assets ratio of 0.6. Calculate and interpret Sysco's Z score.

10. Federal - Mogul Corp. has $6 million in funds to distribute to its unsecured creditors. Three possible sets of unsecured claims are presented. Calculate the settlement, if any, to be received by each creditor in each case shown in the following table.

Unsecured Creditors' claims	Case I	Case ll	Case lll
Unpaid balance of secured mortgage	$2,000,000	$3,000,000	4,000,000
Accounts payable	1,000,000	2,000,000	1,000,000
Notes payable - bank	4,000,000	3,000,000	5,000,000
Debentures	3,000,000	4,000,000	5,000,000
Total	10,000,000	12,000,000	15,000,000

SOLUTIONS

True or False Questions

1. F	6. T
2. F	7. F
3. T	8. T
4. F	9. T
5. F	10. F

Multiple Choice Questions

1. C	6. A
2. B	7. B
3. A	8. A
4. D	9. C
5. C	10. A

Questions and Problems

1. Creditors will accept a plan for reorganization if there is a chance that they will receive more money than under liquidation. Creditors recognize that sometimes a firm needs more time to turn around a business. Furthermore, creditors may be reluctant to write off their debt and recognize a loss or would likely happen in a liquidation.

2. The Altman's Z score is useful to investors because they can predict bankruptcy with a fair degree of accuracy. Then investors can sell the troubled firm before it becomes bankrupt to limit losses. A firm can use the Z score to measure its possibility of bankruptcy, look for causes, and work at correcting problems before the firm becomes financially distressed.

3. At a P/E ratio of 15 times, the earnings are worth 15 x $900,000 = $13.5 million. This value minus the investment of $4 million gives the value of Enron of $9.5 million, which is greater than the liquidation value of $9 million. Therefore, Enron should be reorganized.

4. a. Paying a group 70 cents on the dollar immediately (composition) and paying the remainders 60 cents in installments (composition and extension).

   b. Paying all creditors full in 500 days (extension).

   c. Paying a group of creditors in full over three years (extension) and the rest a percentage immediately (composition).

5. Each creditor is paid 45 cents on the dollar (composition). This will require 0.45 x $20 million = $ 9 million, which is equal to the amount of marketable securities the firm has. Apollo Industries will have $0 value after it pays its creditors.

6. Each creditor will be paid in full in three payments (extension). This will require a payment every nine months. The first payment will be 0.40 x $20 million = $8 million. The second and third payments will be $6 million each. Apollo's $9 million of marketable short-term assets is inadequate to fund this plan.

7. Pay $4 million of claims in full and the remainder at 40 cents on the dollar in 90 days (composition and extension). The firm does not have sufficient cash to meet this payment schedule. It has $9 million and this plan requires $10.4 million [$4 million + ($16 million x 0.4)].

8. Each creditor will be paid 50 cents on the dollar in two quarterly installments (composition and extension). This will require two quarterly payments of $6 million and $4 million, respectively. Apollo's $9 million of marketable short-term assets is inadequate to fund this plan.

9. Altman's $Z = 1.2(X1) + 1.4(X2) + 3.3(X3) + 0.6 (X4) + 1.0 (X5)$

   Where $X1$ = working capital / total assets = 0.3.
            $X2$ = retained earnings / total assets = 0.15.
            $X3$ = EBIT / total assets = 0.1.
            $X4$ = market value of equity / book value of debt = 0.4.
            $X5$ = sales / total assets = 0.6.

   Altman's $Z = (1.2) (0.3) + (1.4) (0.15) + 3.3 (0.1) + 0.6 (0.4) + (1) (0.6)$
            $= 0.36 + 0.21 + 0.33 + 0.24 + 0.6 = 1.74.$

   With a Z score of 1.74, Sysco has a high probability of failure.

10. Assume that each unsecured creditor has equal priority. In case I , each creditor will receive $6 million / $10 million = $0.60 on the dollar. In case ll, each creditor will receive $6 million / $12 million = $0.50 on the dollar. In case lll, each creditor will receive $6 million / $15 million = $0.40 on the dollar. The actual amounts received are as follows:

Unsecured Creditor	Case l	Case ll	Case lll
Second mortgage	$1,200,000	$1,500,000	$1,600,000
Accounts payable	600,000	1,000,000	400,000
Notes payable	2,400,000	1,500,000	2, 000,000
Debentures	1,800,000	2,000,000	2,000,000
	$6,000,000	$6,000,000	$6,000,000